List of Contents

Introduction: Unveiling the Midas Touch Secret: Transforming Business into Goldmines

Welcome, fellow adventurers of the entrepreneurial realm, to a journey that will unravel the enigmatic allure of turning businesses into profit-spewing goldmines. In this voyage through the intricate labyrinth of commerce, I invite you to don your visionary hats, for we are about to explore the depths of a secret that has eluded many, yet has the potential to reshape the destiny of enterprises.

In the age-old myth of King Midas, the mere touch of his hand transmuted all he encountered into shimmering gold. This captivating tale, echoing through the annals of time, finds an intriguing parallel in the art of business. Entrepreneurs often yearn for the touch that can transform their endeavors into boundless profit, and much like Midas, they search for the secret elixir that can turn the mundane into precious prosperity.

The pursuit of profit, though, is not a quest solely for the greedy or materialistic; it is a vital force that fuels the engine of commerce, propelling innovation, creating livelihoods, and fostering progress. It's a symphony of economic chords that, when played harmoniously, produce not just financial gain, but also a harmonious resonance that reverberates across industries and societies.

Before we delve into the depths of the Midas Touch Secret, let us cast aside any preconceived notions. For the secret I'm about to unveil is not an incantation for instant wealth or a magic spell that guarantees boundless riches. It is, in fact, a fusion of timeless wisdom and contemporary strategies, a symposium of proven practices and novel approaches.

Picture a landscape where every business, from the humblest startup to the grandest corporation, possesses the uncanny ability to generate profit without compromise, to thrive in the face of adversity, and to leave a mark that extends beyond the balance sheet. Imagine a realm where profitability is not an elusive chimera, but a wellspring that can be harnessed through strategic acumen and unwavering determination.

The Midas Touch Secret is a tapestry woven from multifaceted threads of knowledge, each thread contributing to the fabric of a thriving business. It is founded upon the bedrock of financial acumen, where understanding profit margins, cash flow dynamics, and sustainable growth forms the cornerstone. But it extends beyond the realm of number-crunching, diving into the depths of human psychology, market dynamics, and the art of resilience.

In our exploration, we shall traverse the landscapes of market analysis, branding alchemy, financial stewardship, and operational finesse. We shall scrutinize the nuances of customer relationships, team dynamics, and the delicate dance between innovation and tradition. The Midas Touch Secret is not a solitary revelation but a constellation of insights, an assemblage of strategies that, when combined, illuminate the path to enduring profitability.

It's imperative to understand that the Midas Touch Secret is not an instant potion; it is a transformative process. Like the metamorphosis of a caterpillar into a butterfly, it requires time, effort, and a commitment to growth. It demands the willingness to adapt, the courage to face challenges, and the humility to learn from failures.

As we embark on this expedition, I urge you to open your minds to the possibilities that lie ahead. Whether you're a seasoned entrepreneur seeking to amplify your enterprise's profitability or an aspiring businessperson setting foot in the world of commerce, the Midas Touch Secret holds the potential to reshape your perspective and invigorate your endeavors.

Throughout this odyssey, we shall decipher the DNA of profitability, dissecting its genes to reveal the blueprint for success. We shall navigate the labyrinth of business intricacies, uncovering hidden treasures of insight and wisdom. We shall embrace the power of innovation, the elegance of strategy, and the tenacity of execution.

Dear reader, it's time to embark on a voyage where the Midas Touch Secret shall be our guiding star, illuminating the path to prosperity. The journey will be profound, the insights transformative, and the revelations empowering. So, arm yourself with curiosity, equip yourself with dedication, and prepare to uncover the secrets that can turn your business ventures into goldmines of prosperity.

The Midas Touch Secret awaits, eager to be unveiled and wielded for the betterment of enterprises and the enrichment of lives. Let us commence this expedition, penning a new chapter in the annals of business success, one touch at a time.

May your ventures shine with the brilliance of gold, and may your journey through these pages bring you closer to the Midas Touch Secret.

Chapter 1: The Foundation of Profitable Business

Understanding Profitability Dynamics

Profitability isn't just a financial metric; it's the lifeblood of a business's sustainability and growth. In this sub-chapter, we will delve into the intricate world of profitability dynamics, exploring the profound importance of profit, dissecting the components of a profit and loss statement, and uncovering the transformative potential of profit margin analysis.

Importance of Profit in Business Sustainability

Profit is the heartbeat of any business, propelling its operations, fueling innovation, and enabling long-term viability. At its core, profit is the surplus remaining after all expenses have been deducted from revenue. While revenue is undoubtedly a vital metric, it's the profit that truly determines the health and resilience of a business.

Profitability serves as a beacon for decision-making. It allows businesses to reinvest in research and development, expand their reach, and withstand economic fluctuations. It empowers entrepreneurs to nurture their ventures, offer competitive salaries to their workforce, and ensure the seamless functioning of their operations. In essence, profit isn't a luxury; it's a necessity that safeguards a business's future.

Components of a Profit and Loss Statement

A profit and loss (P&L) statement, also known as an income statement, is the financial compass that guides a business's profitability journey. It lays bare the financial performance of a business within a specific timeframe, detailing its revenue, expenses, and ultimately, its profit. Understanding the components of a P&L statement is paramount for unraveling the intricate threads that weave the fabric of profitability.

Revenue: The cornerstone of a P&L statement, revenue represents the total amount of money generated from the sale of goods or services. It forms the top line of the statement and serves as the starting point for calculating profitability.

Cost of Goods Sold (COGS): This encompasses the direct costs involved in producing the goods or services sold. It includes expenses like raw materials, manufacturing costs, and labor directly tied to production. Subtracting COGS from revenue yields the gross profit.

Gross Profit: The gross profit represents the amount remaining after deducting COGS from revenue. It reflects the core profitability before considering other operational expenses.

Operating Expenses: These encompass the day-to-day costs of running the business, such as salaries, marketing expenses, rent, utilities, and administrative overheads. Subtracting operating expenses from gross profit yields the operating profit.

Operating Profit: Also known as operating income, this figure represents the profit generated from the core operations of the business before considering interest and taxes.

Interest and Taxes: These are deducted from the operating profit to arrive at the net profit, which is the ultimate measure of profitability.

Profit Margin Analysis for Business Growth
Profit margin analysis goes beyond the surface-level numbers, providing insightful perspectives on a business's efficiency, pricing strategy, and overall financial health. There are several types of profit margins, each shedding light on different aspects of profitability:

Gross Profit Margin: This ratio reveals the percentage of revenue that remains after deducting COGS. A higher gross profit margin indicates effective cost management and pricing strategies.

Operating Profit Margin: Calculated by dividing operating profit by revenue, this margin showcases the efficiency of a business's operations. A higher operating profit margin signifies a greater ability to generate profit from its core activities.

Net Profit Margin: The most comprehensive metric, this margin reflects the percentage of revenue that translates into net profit. It accounts for all expenses, including interest and taxes. A higher net profit margin indicates effective management of all aspects of the business.

In essence, a deeper dive into profit margin analysis unveils areas for improvement, highlights opportunities for cost reduction, and guides strategic decisions that can elevate a business's profitability.

Understanding the dynamics of profitability is not merely a financial exercise; it's the cornerstone of strategic decision-making. Profitability determines a business's ability to innovate, expand, and weather economic storms. By comprehending the components of a profit and loss statement and harnessing the insights from profit margin analysis, entrepreneurs can steer their ventures towards sustainable profitability. In the chapters to come, we'll explore the strategies and tactics that will transform your business into a profit-generating powerhouse.

Identifying Your Business's Unique Value Proposition

In the intricate world of business, where competition is fierce and consumer choices are abundant, the concept of a Unique Value Proposition (USP) stands as a beacon of differentiation and profitability. As we embark on this journey to uncover the Midas Touch Secret to turning any business profitable, it is crucial to lay the cornerstone by delving into the art of crafting a compelling USP.

Defining Your USP (Unique Selling Proposition)

At its essence, the Unique Selling Proposition is the essence of your business distilled into a succinct statement that answers the fundamental question: "Why should customers choose your product or service over the alternatives?" It is the embodiment of what sets your offering apart, the distinct advantage that resonates with your target audience. Your USP is not just a tagline; it's the core promise that captures the hearts and wallets of your customers.

Imagine you're in the market for a new smartphone. In a sea of options, each boasting similar features, what compels you to choose one over the rest? This is where the USP comes into play. For instance, Apple's USP centers around sleek design, user-friendly interfaces, and seamless integration across devices. Tesla's USP revolves around electric vehicles that marry cutting-edge technology with sustainability. Both these examples demonstrate the power of a well-defined USP in shaping consumer preferences.

Aligning Your USP with Market Needs

The next crucial step in refining your USP is aligning it with the ever-evolving needs of your target market. Your business's USP is not set in stone; it should adapt to mirror the shifting desires and demands of your customers. This requires an in-depth understanding of your audience's pain points, aspirations, and behaviors.

Market research becomes your compass in this journey. Through surveys, focus groups, and data analysis, you uncover valuable insights that inform your USP's evolution. For instance, a company that initially positioned itself as a provider of affordable fitness equipment might pivot its USP to emphasize virtual workout experiences during a pandemic, catering to the changing needs of home-bound consumers.

Leveraging Your USP for Competitive Advantage
Once your USP is honed and aligned, its true potency is unveiled when wielded as a competitive advantage. This involves meticulous integration into every facet of your business strategy, from product development to marketing, and from customer service to pricing.

Consider the example of a coffee shop with a USP of offering rare, single-origin coffee beans sourced directly from farmers. To fully leverage this USP, the coffee shop would not only prioritize sourcing and brewing these unique beans but also design its space and marketing campaigns to resonate with the artisanal, coffee-loving audience seeking a distinctive experience.

The key lies in consistency. Your USP should be the common thread that weaves through your brand's narrative, creating a compelling story that customers not only connect with but also become advocates of.

The journey to profitability begins with the formulation of a potent Unique Value Proposition. This carefully crafted statement encapsulates what makes your business extraordinary and why customers should choose you. However, the journey doesn't end here; your USP must constantly evolve to meet the dynamic needs of your market. Moreover, the true alchemy occurs when you seamlessly integrate your USP into every aspect of your business, transforming it into a magnetic force that draws customers, fuels loyalty, and ultimately, paves the path to profitability.

Setting Clear Business Goals for Profit Maximization

In the vast landscape of business, the quest for profitability is akin to the search for hidden treasure. Every entrepreneur dreams of striking gold, turning their business into a beacon of success that not only survives but thrives. However, the journey from inception to profit maximization is marked by strategic planning, unwavering commitment, and perhaps most importantly, the establishment of clear and actionable business goals.

SMART Goal-Setting for Profitability

Imagine embarking on a road trip without a map or GPS. You might have a general direction in mind, but the lack of specific guidance would likely lead to confusion and wasted time. Similarly, in the world of business, setting vague or generic goals is a surefire way to get lost in the complexities of the market. This is where the SMART goal-setting framework emerges as a guiding star.

S - Specific: A profit-oriented goal should be laser-focused and clearly defined. Instead of aiming to "increase profits," a specific goal could be to "increase quarterly net profits by 15% through cost optimization and revenue diversification."

M - Measurable: Tangible metrics are the cornerstone of effective goal-setting. If you can't measure it, you can't manage it. Employing quantifiable metrics such as revenue growth, profit margins, or customer acquisition rates enables precise tracking of progress.

A - Achievable: While audacious goals can inspire greatness, they must also be rooted in reality. Aim for a balance between ambition and feasibility. Consider the resources, expertise, and time required to achieve the goal without sacrificing quality or sustainability.

R - Relevant: Align goals with the broader business strategy and market trends. A relevant goal should contribute to the long-term success of the business and address current challenges or opportunities.

T - Time-Bound: Time is money, and setting a deadline adds urgency and accountability to the goal. Defining a clear timeframe—be it a quarter, a year, or longer—provides a sense of purpose and a framework for progress evaluation.

Short-Term vs. Long-Term Profit Objectives
In the pursuit of profitability, businesses often grapple with the question of whether to prioritize short-term gains or invest in long-term strategies. The answer lies in a nuanced balance that acknowledges the importance of both horizons.

Short-term profit objectives are akin to low-hanging fruit—quick wins that can inject immediate financial relief. These might involve streamlining operational processes, reducing overhead costs, or optimizing pricing strategies. While short-term goals can provide an instant boost to the bottom line, they should never be pursued at the expense of sustainable growth.

Long-term profit objectives, on the other hand, encompass strategies that lay the foundation for enduring success. This could involve product innovation, market expansion, brand-building, and fostering customer loyalty. Such objectives require patience and continuous investment, as the fruits of long-term strategies often take time to ripen.

Monitoring Progress and Adapting Goals Accordingly
Setting goals is only the beginning; monitoring progress and adapting goals as circumstances evolve are equally crucial. In the fast-paced world of business, the landscape can change swiftly. Market trends, consumer preferences, technological advancements, and even unforeseen crises can impact the trajectory of a business.

Regular progress tracking allows you to stay on course and make informed decisions. Whether through key performance indicators (KPIs), financial reports, or data analysis, having a finger on the pulse of your business ensures that you can celebrate victories, identify bottlenecks, and make timely adjustments.

Adaptability is the secret sauce of successful goal-setting. If market dynamics shift or if certain strategies don't yield the expected results, be willing to recalibrate your goals. This doesn't indicate failure; rather, it showcases your agility and commitment to optimizing profitability.

Setting clear business goals for profit maximization is the cornerstone of sustainable success. The SMART framework empowers you to establish goals that are specific, measurable, achievable, relevant, and time-bound. Balancing short-term gains with long-term strategies provides a well-rounded approach to profitability. Lastly, monitoring progress and adapting goals in response to changing circumstances ensures that your business remains on a path of growth and prosperity. Remember, in the realm of business, setting the right goals is akin to discovering the treasure map that guides you toward the Midas touch of profitability.

Chapter 2: Market Analysis and Customer Segmentation

Conducting Comprehensive Market Research

In the dynamic landscape of modern business, the compass that guides success is market research. It's not just about having a brilliant idea or a groundbreaking product; it's about understanding the intricate interplay of market forces and consumer behaviors that can propel your business toward profitability. In this sub chapter, we delve deep into the art and science of comprehensive market research, an essential pillar of the Midas Touch Secret for turning any business into a profitable venture.

Gathering Insights into Market Trends and Demands

Market trends are the footprints of consumer preferences, the ripples on the vast ocean of demand. To harness these trends and steer your business toward profitability, you must immerse yourself in the currents of the market. The process begins with identifying the megatrends that shape industries and trickle down to affect businesses of all sizes. Stay attuned to demographic shifts, cultural changes, and technological advancements that are rewriting the rules of engagement.

Beyond the macro trends, micro trends are the nuances that distinguish your target market. What drives consumer decisions? What are the pain points they seek to alleviate? By observing purchasing patterns and listening to the whispers of social media, you can gain profound insights into the motivations behind consumer choices. By understanding what they want and why they want it, you're positioning your business on the path to profitability.

Analyzing Competitors and Identifying Gaps
In the grand tapestry of the market, competitors are the other threads that your business must navigate through. Competitor analysis isn't about replication; it's about differentiation. Through a comprehensive analysis of your competitors, you uncover the gaps in the market that your business is uniquely positioned to fill. What are your competitors doing right? What are their weaknesses? How can your business offer something superior, more innovative, or simply different?

Remember, these gaps are the fertile grounds where profitability sprouts. By identifying the untapped needs and unmet desires, you're crafting a roadmap that leads to your business becoming the go-to solution. But this is not merely about comparison; it's about gaining inspiration, spotting opportunities, and sculpting your value proposition to shine in the spotlight of differentiation.

Research Techniques for Accurate Data Collection
Data, in the age of information, is the currency of precision. It is the bedrock on which strategic decisions are made. Collecting accurate data is like prospecting for gold in the digital mines. And much like a prospector, you need the right tools and techniques to extract the valuable nuggets.

Surveys, focus groups, and interviews are time-tested methods for tapping into the minds of your potential customers. The insights gained here can be invaluable, providing firsthand accounts of pain points, preferences, and desires. In the digital realm, web analytics offer a treasure trove of information, revealing the paths customers take on your website, the pages they linger on, and the ones they abandon.

Additionally, the advent of big data and AI has opened new vistas. By analyzing massive datasets, you can unveil patterns and correlations that might remain hidden to the naked eye. These insights are the secret sauce, the refined gold that empowers you to make data-driven decisions, refine your strategies, and mold your offerings to meet the unspoken needs of your market.

Conducting comprehensive market research is not just a box to check off; it's an ongoing journey that connects you intimately with your market and customers. It's the process that transforms your business from a mere participant to a market leader, from a struggling venture to a profitable endeavor. By immersing yourself in market trends, understanding your competitors, and harnessing the power of accurate data, you're uncovering the secrets that will turn your business into a shining example of the Midas Touch in action.

Segmenting Your Target Audience Effectively

In the dynamic landscape of modern business, the pursuit of profitability is a journey that requires astute navigation through a sea of potential customers. The concept of "one size fits all" has long been relegated to the annals of business history, replaced by a more nuanced approach: customer segmentation. In this sub-chapter, we delve into the profound significance of customer segmentation for enhancing profitability, explore the diverse criteria employed for effective segmentation, and unravel the art of tailoring products and services to resonate with specific customer segments.

Importance of Customer Segmentation for Profitability

Imagine embarking on a journey without a map; a venture into the unknown without any guidance. This analogy aptly illustrates the folly of neglecting customer segmentation in the business world. The realm of customers is not a homogenous expanse; it's a rich mosaic of individuals with varying needs, preferences, and behaviors. By grouping these individuals into segments based on shared characteristics, businesses gain invaluable insights into what drives these segments to make purchasing decisions.

Customer segmentation is the compass that guides businesses towards profitable shores. It enables them to channel resources effectively, streamline marketing efforts, and provide tailored solutions that resonate with specific groups. Instead of casting a wide net and hoping to catch a few fish, businesses can laser-focus their strategies, reducing wastage and maximizing returns.

Different Segmentation Criteria
The art of customer segmentation is multi-dimensional, encompassing a variety of criteria that help businesses divide their customer base into meaningful groups. Demographic segmentation considers attributes such as age, gender, income, and education. This provides a fundamental understanding of the basic characteristics of customers and lays the foundation for more intricate segmentation strategies.

Psychographic segmentation delves deeper, examining the psychological and behavioral aspects of customers. This includes their lifestyle, values, interests, and personality traits. By understanding what makes customers tick on a psychological level, businesses can align their offerings with customers' aspirations and values.

Geographic segmentation capitalizes on the physical locations of customers, taking into account factors such as location, climate, and cultural nuances. This is particularly relevant for global businesses, as it helps tailor strategies to suit the unique needs of specific regions.

Behavioral segmentation hinges on customers' interactions with a business. This could encompass their purchase history, frequency of interaction, loyalty, and response to marketing efforts. Understanding these behaviors allows businesses to craft personalized experiences that resonate and drive conversion.

Tailoring Products/Services to Specific Customer Segments

Once the tapestry of customer segments is woven, the next step involves tailoring products and services to cater to the unique preferences and needs of each group. This is not a mere exercise in superficial customization; it's about crafting offerings that genuinely add value and resonate with customers on a profound level.

Let's consider an example. A company operating in the fitness industry might discover through segmentation that they have two primary customer segments: young professionals seeking convenience and older adults seeking health improvement. For the first segment, they might introduce an app-based workout program that fits seamlessly into busy schedules. For the second segment, they could offer personalized training sessions that focus on joint health and mobility.

This tailored approach not only enhances customer satisfaction but also fosters loyalty and advocacy. When customers feel that a business understands their unique needs and is committed to meeting them, they are more likely to become loyal patrons and enthusiastic brand advocates.

Customer segmentation is not a mere business strategy; it's an art form that transforms raw data into profound insights, enabling businesses to resonate deeply with their customers. By embracing segmentation, businesses can navigate the vast sea of potential customers with precision, charting a course that leads to profitability. Through demographic, psychographic, geographic, and behavioral lenses, they can unlock the key to each segment's desires. And by tailoring products and services to cater to these desires, businesses can create relationships that are not just transactional but transformative. The journey to profitability is paved with the stones of customer segmentation; every step taken along this path brings businesses closer to the treasure trove of success.

Creating Customer Personas for Targeted Marketing

In the intricate tapestry of the business world, one thread stands out prominently – the customer. Every successful business owes its triumph to a deep understanding of its customers' desires, preferences, and behaviors. This sub chapter delves into the art of crafting customer personas, a masterstroke in the symphony of targeted marketing. By unveiling the layers of this strategic approach, we unveil the key to forging meaningful connections and driving customer loyalty.

Developing Detailed Customer Personas

Imagine having a conversation with a friend. To connect on a deeper level, you seek to understand their aspirations, challenges, and preferences. Similarly, in the realm of business, crafting customer personas involves creating fictional representations of your ideal customers. These personas are rich in details that extend beyond mere demographics, encompassing psychographics, behaviors, and pain points.

Begin by gathering data from various sources—customer surveys, social media insights, and purchase history. Identify patterns and commonalities, and categorize your customers into distinct segments. Assign each segment a name, profession, family background, hobbies, and even a backstory. The goal is to humanize these personas, making them relatable characters with specific needs and aspirations. Dive deeper into psychographic information – unraveling the tapestry of motivations, aspirations, and pain points. This holistic view paints a vivid picture of who your customers truly are.

Imagine "Alex the Adventurer," a persona that emerges from your analysis. Alex, a 28-year-old tech enthusiast, seeks innovative solutions that simplify life's complexities. With a penchant for sustainability, Alex's buying decisions are driven by a desire to make a positive impact. This level of detail enables you to tailor your marketing efforts to resonate deeply with Alex's values and goals.

Mapping Customer Journeys for Better Engagement
With your customer personas in hand, it's time to embark
on the journey they take when interacting with your
business. Mapping customer journeys involves
understanding each persona's touchpoints—from the initial
awareness of your product or service to post-purchase
interactions.

Consider a tech-savvy young professional named Alex,
who is always on the lookout for innovative gadgets. Alex's
journey might start with social media exposure to your
product, followed by thorough online research,
comparisons, and finally, the purchase decision.
Understanding this journey allows you to tailor your
marketing efforts, ensuring that the right information is
available at each stage to facilitate Alex's decision-making
process.

Personalization Strategies to Increase Customer Loyalty
In a world where attention is a prized commodity,
personalization emerges as the secret weapon to capture
and retain customer loyalty. By tailoring your interactions
to match individual preferences, you create an emotional
bond that transcends transactional relationships.
Personalization is the art of making each customer feel like
your business was designed exclusively for them.

Leverage data and technology to personalize experiences.
Use purchase history to recommend complementary
products, send personalized emails addressing the customer
by name, or even create unique landing pages that cater to

specific personas. Netflix, for instance, personalizes its homepage based on users' viewing history, ensuring a seamless and enjoyable content discovery experience.

Personalization extends beyond products—it's about understanding your customers' values and needs. If one of your personas is a health-conscious parent, your communications could highlight the health benefits of your offerings and how they align with family values.

Crafting customer personas, mapping their journeys, and implementing personalized strategies are essential pillars of successful modern marketing. It's the bridge that connects businesses with their audience on a human level, fostering a connection that extends beyond transactional interactions. As a business owner, take the time to delve deep into the minds and hearts of your customers. By doing so, you'll not only drive profitability but also create a lasting impact that resonates far beyond the bottom line.

Chapter 3: Crafting a Profit-Driven Business Strategy

Designing a Value-Centric Business Model

In the dynamic landscape of modern business, crafting a profit-driven strategy is not just a choice; it's a necessity for sustained success. At the heart of such a strategy lies a value-centric business model, an intricate web of decisions and structures that can transform an ordinary enterprise into a profit powerhouse. In this sub-chapter, we will delve into the art of designing a value-centric business model, exploring the diverse array of business models available, understanding the nuances of value creation, and learning the delicate dance of balancing revenue streams for consistent profitability.

Exploring Various Business Models

Every business begins with a spark of innovation, a concept that holds the promise of solving a problem or fulfilling a need. Yet, the journey from concept to profitability requires a carefully chosen business model—a blueprint that outlines how the company will generate revenue, deliver value to customers, and ultimately thrive. The landscape of business models is as diverse as it is intriguing, with options ranging from traditional retail and service-based models to innovative subscription and freemium models.

The subscription model, for instance, has gained immense popularity in recent years. It hinges on providing customers with ongoing value in exchange for a regular fee. This model fosters loyalty, establishes recurring revenue streams, and creates a steady foundation for profit growth. Consider the success of subscription-based services like streaming platforms and software-as-a-service (SaaS) providers; their models prioritize continuous value delivery and long-term customer relationships.

On the other hand, freemium models offer a taste of value for free, enticing customers to upgrade to premium tiers for enhanced features or services. This approach effectively lowers the entry barrier for customers and taps into the psychology of reciprocity—a potential customer is more likely to engage further after experiencing initial value. This model can foster rapid user acquisition, laying the groundwork for profitable expansion.

Incorporating Value Creation at Every Touchpoint
In the realm of business, value creation isn't a one-time event; it's a constant journey that extends across every touchpoint between the company and its customers. Designing a value-centric business model involves deeply understanding your customers' pain points, desires, and aspirations. What problems are you solving? How are you making your customers' lives easier, more enjoyable, or more productive? These questions are the cornerstones of a value-driven approach.

Value isn't just about your products or services; it's about the entire customer experience. This includes user-friendly interfaces, efficient processes, timely customer support, and meaningful engagement. Consider the success of companies like Apple, which not only delivers innovative products but also provides a seamless, enjoyable experience from the moment customers step into an Apple Store to the day they unbox their new device.

Balancing Revenue Streams for Consistent Profit
A well-constructed business model is a tapestry of revenue streams, each contributing to the overall profitability of the enterprise. A common pitfall is relying too heavily on a single revenue source, making the business vulnerable to fluctuations in that specific market. To ensure consistent profit, it's essential to diversify revenue streams while ensuring they align with your value proposition and customer base.

For instance, a company might have multiple product lines catering to different customer segments. These segments might have varying preferences and purchasing behaviors. By catering to diverse needs, the company mitigates the risk of relying solely on one product's success. Additionally, exploring complementary revenue streams, such as licensing, partnerships, or affiliate marketing, can add stability to your business's financial landscape.

Crafting a value-centric business model is the linchpin of a profit-driven strategy. By exploring diverse business models, intricately weaving value creation into every touchpoint, and carefully balancing revenue streams, a business can position itself for sustained success and profitability. Remember, a business model is not static; it should evolve as your market, customers, and technologies do. Embrace the challenge of innovation, for therein lies the path to the Midas touch of profitability.

SWOT Analysis for Strategic Decision Making

In the realm of business strategy, the ability to discern the terrain upon which your enterprise stands is tantamount to success. Just as a seasoned general surveys the battlefield before committing to a strategy, so must a business leader embark upon an informed course of action. One of the most potent tools in this arsenal of strategic decision-making is the SWOT analysis. Derived from the acronym for Strengths, Weaknesses, Opportunities, and Threats, the SWOT analysis unfurls a panoramic view of both the internal and external factors that can shape a business's trajectory. In this sub-chapter, we delve into the intricacies of SWOT analysis, unveiling its profound influence on crafting a profit-driven business strategy.

Assessing Internal Strengths and Weaknesses

Peering within the walls of your organization is an essential preamble to effective decision-making. Herein lies the core tenet of assessing internal strengths and weaknesses through the lens of a SWOT analysis. Strengths encompass the bedrock attributes that set your business apart - the unique resources, expertise, and competitive advantages that grant your enterprise a distinct edge in the market. It could be your top-tier talent pool, cutting-edge technology, or a renowned brand that engenders customer loyalty.

Strengths may manifest in various forms: a dedicated and skilled workforce, proprietary technology, a well-established brand, or efficient operational processes. It's these strengths that can become key drivers of competitive advantage.

On the converse, weaknesses cast a light on the aspects that require fortification or transformation. They might span from operational inefficiencies to gaps in skills or lackluster customer service. Candidly acknowledging these vulnerabilities becomes a foundation upon which growth is predicated.

Evaluating External Opportunities and Threats
No business operates within a vacuum; external forces exert substantial influence. This is where the second duo of the SWOT equation - Opportunities and Threats - assumes its significance. Opportunities unfurl as latent prospects, uncharted avenues, and emerging trends that could catapult your business to new heights. It could be a burgeoning market segment, an untapped demographic, or an unexplored geographic territory. Identifying and seizing these opportunities necessitates keen observation and an innate entrepreneurial spirit.

Conversely, threats emerge as the spectral figures that loom over your business's horizon. They encompass competitive pressures, shifting consumer behaviors, technological disruptions, and regulatory changes that could erode your market share or profitability. A comprehensive SWOT analysis casts a discerning eye on these external factors, unveiling potential roadblocks and allowing your strategic compass to navigate past them.

Formulating Strategies Based on SWOT Insights
The culmination of dissecting internal strengths and weaknesses and evaluating external opportunities and threats culminates in the formulation of strategies that harness the full spectrum of insights gleaned from the SWOT analysis. Crafting a profit-driven business strategy necessitates aligning the internal fortifications with the external pursuits.

For instance, if your analysis reveals a formidable strength in technological innovation, a corresponding strategy might involve harnessing this strength to capitalize on an emerging market opportunity. On the flip side, if a glaring weakness in supply chain management is identified, a strategic imperative would be to bolster these operations, thereby fortifying your business against potential threats that could arise from disruptions.

Furthermore, the synergy between these strategies generates a roadmap for tactical execution. Each strength is harnessed, each weakness mitigated, every opportunity seized, and each threat averted, all orchestrated towards the crescendo of profitability.

In the grand tapestry of business, the SWOT analysis stands as a mosaic, offering a composite view that guides business leaders toward the zenith of strategic prowess. It is an instrument that empowers them to transform weaknesses into strengths, threats into opportunities, and aspirations into reality. By interlacing these insights into the fabric of the larger business strategy, one crafts a blueprint that doesn't just strive for profit but engineers it. The SWOT analysis isn't merely a tool; it's a lodestar that navigates a business through the tempestuous waters of uncertainty, transforming every decision into a calculated stride towards profitability.

Building a Scalable Infrastructure for Profit Scaling

In the world of business, growth is not just a goal; it's a necessity. As the demand for your products or services increases, your ability to meet that demand while maintaining profitability becomes paramount. This is where scalability comes into play—a concept that separates the thriving businesses from those that falter under the weight of success. In this sub-chapter, we will explore the profound importance of scalability in profit growth, the strategic investment in technology and automation, and the delicate art of scaling operations without compromising quality.

Importance of Scalability in Profit Growth

Scalability is the ability of a business to handle increased workloads, deliver consistent quality, and meet customer demands efficiently, all while preserving or enhancing profit margins. In essence, it's about creating a business framework that can be expanded or contracted as needed, like a well-tuned orchestra that can seamlessly accommodate more instruments without missing a beat. Scalability isn't just about accommodating growth; it's about embracing growth as a mechanism to amplify profits.

For modern businesses, scalability is not optional—it's a strategic imperative. As markets evolve and customer expectations shift, the business that can adapt swiftly gains a competitive edge. Scalability allows you to capture new opportunities without being bogged down by the constraints that hinder growth. It ensures that your operations remain agile, costs are contained, and profits continue to rise in harmony with expansion.

Investing in Technology and Automation

In the realm of scalability, technology and automation are the dynamic duo that fuels growth. The investment in advanced systems and software is more than just a modern luxury; it's a cornerstone of profitability. Automation streamlines processes, eliminates manual bottlenecks, reduces errors, and enhances efficiency across the board. It allows your business to handle increased volume without proportionally increasing costs.

Imagine a customer service department that can handle twice the inquiries without doubling its staff. Picture an inventory management system that adjusts stock levels automatically based on real-time sales data, minimizing excess and shortages. These are the transformative powers of technology and automation at work. By integrating these tools into your business operations, you're not only preparing for growth but actively inviting it.

Scaling Operations Without Compromising Quality
One of the common concerns when scaling a business is the potential dilution of quality. As you increase output, the fear is that attention to detail and customer satisfaction might suffer. This concern is not unwarranted, as many businesses have stumbled at this very juncture. However, scaling without compromising quality is a delicate balancing act that can be achieved with meticulous planning and the right mindset.

Quality is the cornerstone of customer loyalty, and scaling should never undermine it. The key lies in establishing robust processes and protocols that ensure consistent quality standards are met, regardless of volume. Training and empowering your workforce to maintain these standards is crucial. Additionally, constant monitoring and feedback loops can help you identify any drop in quality before it becomes a glaring issue.

Moreover, scaling can actually improve quality through increased specialization. With more resources at your disposal, you can allocate experts to specific tasks, ensuring that each aspect of your business is handled by someone who excels at it. This not only enhances quality but also boosts efficiency and customer satisfaction.

Building a scalable infrastructure is not an option; it's a strategic imperative for profit scaling. By embracing scalability, investing in technology and automation, and maintaining a laser focus on quality, you set the stage for not just growth, but sustainable and profitable growth. As you embark on this journey, remember that scalability is not just about expanding your business—it's about creating a symphony of success where profit crescendos as your business reaches new heights.

Chapter 4: Effective Marketing Strategies for Profitability

Developing a Results-Driven Marketing Plan

In the world of business, where competition is fierce and markets are ever-evolving, a well-crafted marketing plan is akin to a compass guiding a ship through tumultuous waters. Just as a ship's captain sets a course with clear objectives, a business must develop a results-driven marketing plan to navigate its way to profitability. In this sub chapter, we delve into the intricacies of crafting a marketing plan that not only paves the way for success but also ensures a substantial return on investment (ROI).

Crafting Clear Marketing Objectives

The foundation of a successful marketing plan lies in the clarity of its objectives. Just as a ship captain needs a destination, a business needs well-defined goals to steer its marketing efforts. Effective objectives are SMART: Specific, Measurable, Achievable, Relevant, and Time-bound. By articulating specific objectives, businesses can focus their resources and efforts on precisely what they aim to achieve.

For instance, rather than a vague goal of "increasing sales," a SMART objective could be "achieving a 15% increase in online sales within the next quarter." This specificity empowers teams to align their strategies, from product development to campaign execution, toward a common target.

Selecting Appropriate Marketing Channels

In the digital age, where consumers are scattered across various online platforms, selecting the right marketing channels is paramount. Each channel serves as a medium to reach and engage with your target audience effectively. The key lies in understanding your audience's preferences, behaviors, and habits.

From social media platforms to search engines, email marketing to content marketing, every channel has its strengths and limitations. For instance, a visually appealing product might benefit from a strong presence on platforms like Instagram, while a B2B service might find better traction through LinkedIn. A thorough analysis of your audience and market will guide your channel selection, ensuring that your message reaches the right eyes and ears.

Allocating Resources Efficiently for Maximum ROI

A marketing plan, no matter how meticulously designed, can only thrive if supported by the right resources. Just as a ship needs fuel to stay on course, your marketing endeavors require financial, human, and technological resources to succeed. Allocating resources efficiently is the cornerstone of achieving maximum ROI.

Resource allocation involves a delicate balance. While it's tempting to overspend in pursuit of aggressive marketing goals, it's equally important to avoid unnecessary expenditure that doesn't contribute to the desired outcomes. A comprehensive budget that considers various marketing initiatives and allocates resources based on expected impact is indispensable.

Moreover, wise resource allocation extends to human capital. Skilled marketers, copywriters, designers, and data analysts are the crew members who ensure your marketing ship sails smoothly. Hiring the right talent, providing ongoing training, and fostering a culture of creativity and collaboration will contribute significantly to the effectiveness of your marketing efforts.

Developing a results-driven marketing plan is the compass that guides a business toward profitable shores. By crafting clear marketing objectives, selecting appropriate channels, and allocating resources efficiently, a business can set sail with confidence, knowing that every marketing effort is aligned with a purpose and poised to deliver significant ROI.

Implementing Content Marketing for Profitable Engagement

As business landscapes evolve in the digital age, conventional marketing strategies have given way to a more dynamic and customer-centric approach—content marketing. Content marketing has emerged as a powerful tool that not only drives profitable engagement but also establishes a brand's authority and fosters lasting customer relationships. In this sub-chapter, we delve into the art and science of content marketing, exploring how businesses can create, leverage, and optimize valuable content to enhance profitability and create a significant impact.

Creating Valuable and Relevant Content
At the heart of successful content marketing lies the creation of valuable and relevant content that resonates with the target audience. In a sea of information, consumers are drawn to content that addresses their needs, concerns, and aspirations. To achieve this, businesses must embark on a journey of understanding their audience—its demographics, pain points, and preferences. Armed with this knowledge, brands can tailor their content to offer solutions, insights, or entertainment that add genuine value to the lives of their customers.

The cornerstone of valuable content is authenticity. Authenticity breeds trust, and trust is the bedrock upon which profitable customer relationships are built. Whether it's through informative blog posts, engaging videos, or thought-provoking podcasts, businesses must focus on creating content that reflects their brand's voice, aligns with their core values, and speaks directly to their audience's interests.

Leveraging Content to Build Brand Authority
In the digital era, brand authority is a prized currency. It signifies expertise, credibility, and a commitment to

providing value. Content marketing is a strategic avenue for brands to establish and solidify their authority within their industry. By consistently delivering high-quality content that educates, informs, and entertains, businesses position themselves as thought leaders, capturing the attention of their target audience and commanding respect in their field.

To leverage content effectively for brand authority, a deliberate approach is crucial. This involves:

1. In-depth Research: Develop content that goes beyond the surface. Dive into industry trends, emerging technologies, and relevant topics that demonstrate a profound understanding of the subject matter.

2. Original Insights: Offer fresh perspectives and insights that provoke thought and generate discussions. This not only captures attention but also encourages audience engagement.

3. Consistency: Establish a content calendar and maintain regularity in content delivery. Consistency reinforces your brand's commitment to providing valuable information over time.

Measuring Content Performance and Optimizing Strategies
Creating content is just the first step; measuring its impact is equally critical. This entails analyzing various metrics to gauge how effectively your content resonates with the audience and contributes to profitability. Metrics to

consider include website traffic, social media engagement, time spent on pages, conversion rates, and audience demographics.

Understanding these metrics provides actionable insights into what's working and what isn't. It helps in identifying the type of content that drives the most engagement and conversions, enabling businesses to allocate resources effectively. Furthermore, tracking performance over time helps in adapting strategies to changing audience preferences and market dynamics.

Optimizing content strategies is an ongoing process. Based on performance analysis, businesses can refine their approach by:

1. Content Personalization: Tailor content to different segments of your audience. Personalized content speaks directly to individual needs and increases engagement.

2. Experimentation: Test different formats, such as videos, infographics, and case studies, to identify the most effective content types for your audience.

3. SEO Optimization: Incorporate relevant keywords and phrases to improve search engine visibility. This ensures that your valuable content reaches the right audience.

Content marketing has evolved into a cornerstone of effective marketing strategies. By creating valuable and

relevant content, leveraging it to build brand authority, and
consistently measuring and optimizing strategies,
businesses can harness the power of content to engage
customers profitably. In the digital age, content is not just
king—it's a strategic pathway to the hearts and wallets of
your target audience.

Leveraging Data Analytics for Informed Marketing Decisions

In the digital age, where every click, interaction, and
transaction leaves a trail of data, the ability to harness and
analyze this information has become a pivotal factor in
devising effective marketing strategies. Data analytics has
transformed marketing from an art based on intuition to a
science driven by insights. In this sub-chapter, we delve
into the profound significance of data-driven marketing
insights, explore the utilization of key performance
indicators (KPIs), and delve into the art of A/B testing as a
means to fine-tune and optimize marketing campaigns for
maximum profitability.

The Power of Data-Driven Marketing Insights

Data has emerged as the modern-day currency of business,
providing a window into the minds and behaviors of
consumers. Data-driven marketing revolves around
extracting actionable insights from this avalanche of
information. It's not just about understanding what

happened; it's about discerning why it happened and, more importantly, what's likely to happen next.

The central ethos of data-driven marketing is to make decisions grounded in evidence rather than assumptions. This practice involves collecting and analyzing data across various touchpoints – from social media engagement to website visits, and from email click-through rates to customer purchase patterns. By deciphering these data points, businesses can understand their customers on a deeper level, uncover hidden trends, and anticipate future needs.

Unveiling Key Performance Indicators (KPIs)
Key Performance Indicators (KPIs) are the compass that guides marketing strategies. These quantifiable metrics serve as markers of success and provide a tangible measure of the effectiveness of various marketing efforts. KPIs vary depending on business objectives, industry, and specific campaign goals.

For instance, an e-commerce business might focus on conversion rates, tracking the percentage of website visitors who make a purchase. A content-based website, on the other hand, might emphasize engagement metrics like time spent on page or the number of pages viewed per session. KPIs not only help gauge the performance of campaigns but also offer insights into what aspects of the strategy need improvement.

A/B Testing: The Art of Data Refinement

In the dynamic world of marketing, assumptions are often proven wrong or right through experimentation. This is where A/B testing steps in as a powerful tool. A/B testing involves comparing two variations of a marketing element to ascertain which one performs better. Whether it's testing different headlines, visuals, or calls to action, A/B testing removes guesswork and replaces it with concrete evidence.

Let's consider an example: An e-commerce retailer wants to optimize its email campaign. It creates two versions of the email, with the only difference being the subject line. By sending each version to a separate segment of the mailing list and analyzing which version generates higher open rates, the retailer can make an informed decision on the more effective subject line.

A/B testing extends to various marketing elements, including landing pages, ad creatives, and even pricing strategies. By systematically testing different variables, marketers can fine-tune their approach based on real-world data, leading to incremental improvements that can significantly impact the bottom line.

The Integration of Data, KPIs, and A/B Testing: A Profitability Symphony

The synergy between data analytics, KPIs, and A/B testing forms a harmonious symphony that drives marketing strategies towards profitability. Let's illustrate this with an example from the hospitality industry:

A hotel chain aims to increase its online bookings. It starts by analyzing data from its website and social media platforms to understand customer preferences and behavior. This data-driven insight reveals that visitors respond positively to personalized offers based on their travel history.

With this insight in mind, the hotel establishes KPIs focused on conversion rates for personalized offers. It designs two variations of an email campaign, one highlighting room discounts and the other emphasizing additional amenities. Through A/B testing, the hotel sends these versions to separate segments of its email list.

Upon analysis, the hotel discovers that the version emphasizing additional amenities leads to a significantly higher conversion rate. Armed with this data, the hotel fine-tunes its marketing strategy to create more personalized offers highlighting amenities. Consequently, online bookings increase, and the hotel's profitability grows.

Unleashing the Power of Data-Driven Marketing
In the realm of modern business, where every decision is being increasingly guided by data, the art of data-driven marketing has become a linchpin in the pursuit of profitability. By deciphering the insights hidden within the data, businesses gain a profound understanding of their customers, enabling them to tailor strategies that resonate and engage.

Key Performance Indicators (KPIs) transform vague aspirations into measurable goals, while A/B testing injects empirical evidence into the decision-making process. Together, this triumvirate of data, KPIs, and A/B testing provides a systematic and evidence-based approach to marketing, ensuring that strategies are not just functional but truly optimized for maximum profitability.

The era of relying on instincts and hunches has given way to a data-driven revolution. As you embark on your journey to craft marketing strategies that wield the Midas touch of profitability, remember that data is not just a collection of numbers—it's the narrative of your customers' desires, the blueprint for effective strategies, and the compass that leads your business toward prosperity. Harness it wisely, and watch as your marketing efforts evolve from educated guesses to informed decisions that drive your business forward.

Chapter 5: Financial Management for Sustainable Profit

Mastering the Basics of Financial Literacy

In the intricate dance of business, financial literacy is the compass that guides entrepreneurs through the tumultuous waters of profit and loss. Understanding the nuances of financial statements, deciphering complex ratios, and mastering the art of budgeting are the cornerstones upon which every successful business is built. Welcome to the realm of financial literacy, where the language of numbers paints a vivid picture of your business's health and prosperity.

Understanding Financial Statements: Unveiling the Financial Canvas

Financial statements are the canvas upon which your business's financial narrative is painted. The most crucial among these are the balance sheet and the cash flow statement. The balance sheet offers a snapshot of your company's financial position at a specific point in time. It showcases your assets, liabilities, and equity, providing insights into your financial stability and solvency.

Imagine your balance sheet as a scale; on one side, you have your assets, the resources your business owns – from cash and inventory to equipment and property. On the other side, you have your liabilities, the obligations your business owes to creditors and stakeholders. The balance between these two sides reveals your equity, the residual interest of the business owner. By analyzing the balance sheet, you gain insights into your liquidity, leverage, and overall financial structure.

Complementing the balance sheet is the cash flow statement, which tracks the inflow and outflow of cash during a specific period. Cash is the lifeblood of any business, and this statement provides clarity on how cash is generated and spent. It categorizes cash flows into operating, investing, and financing activities, illuminating your business's ability to generate cash from its core operations, invest wisely, and raise capital efficiently.

Reading Financial Ratios: Diagnosing Business Health
Financial ratios are the diagnostic tools that reveal the pulse of your business. These ratios distill complex financial data into easy-to-understand metrics, helping you assess your business's health and performance. One of the most critical ratios is the liquidity ratio, which evaluates your company's ability to meet short-term obligations. The current ratio, for instance, compares current assets to current liabilities, reflecting your ability to cover short-term debts.

Another indispensable ratio is profitability ratios, which measure the company's ability to generate profit relative to sales, assets, and equity. The gross profit margin, for instance, gauges the efficiency of your production processes, while the return on equity (ROE) assesses how effectively your business employs shareholders' equity to generate returns.

Efficiency ratios provide insights into how well you manage your assets and liabilities. The inventory turnover ratio reveals how quickly your inventory is sold and replaced, and the receivables turnover ratio measures how effectively you collect outstanding debts from customers.

Budgeting and Managing Cash Flow: The Financial Compass

Cash flow is the rhythm of business – it's the ebb and flow of resources that sustains your operations, fuels growth, and safeguards against downturns. Effective budgeting and cash flow management are like a financial compass, guiding your business toward sustainable profit.

Budgeting is the art of planning and allocating resources based on your business's objectives. It's a roadmap that aligns your financial decisions with your strategic goals. By forecasting revenues and expenses, you gain a forward-looking perspective that aids decision-making and resource allocation. A well-crafted budget enables you to allocate funds strategically, identify potential cash shortages, and make necessary adjustments before they escalate into problems.

Managing cash flow requires meticulous attention to both inflows and outflows. It's not just about increasing sales; it's about ensuring that the revenue you generate arrives in a timely manner. This involves managing accounts receivable, negotiating favorable payment terms, and incentivizing early payments. On the expenditure side, optimizing payment schedules, negotiating discounts with suppliers, and managing overhead costs contribute to cash flow efficiency.

Mastering the basics of financial literacy is akin to deciphering the language of business. It empowers you to decode the financial story your business tells, evaluate its health through ratios, and navigate the unpredictable seas of cash flow. Remember, financial literacy is not a destination but a journey of continuous learning and refinement. As a wise entrepreneur once said, "A business that makes nothing but money is a poor business." By embracing financial literacy, you'll not only make money but also build a robust and enduring business that thrives in the ever-evolving landscape of commerce.

Strategies for Cost Control and Profit Enhancement

As a shrewd business leader, you understand that in the realm of profitability, every penny counts. In today's volatile and competitive market, mastering the art of cost control and profit enhancement can be the key differentiator between a thriving business and a struggling one. In this sub-chapter, we delve into the intricate strategies that can guide your business toward not only identifying and reducing unnecessary costs but also optimizing operations for efficient resource allocation and favorable supplier negotiations.

Identifying and Reducing Unnecessary Costs

Every business, no matter how well-established, can fall into the trap of operational inefficiencies that lead to wasted resources. Identifying these inefficiencies requires a meticulous review of your processes, resources, and expenditures. One of the most effective approaches is conducting a comprehensive cost analysis. This involves categorizing your expenses into fixed, variable, and semi-variable costs.

Fixed costs remain constant regardless of production or sales levels—examples include rent, utilities, and salaries. Variable costs fluctuate with production or sales—raw materials, packaging, and direct labor fall under this category. Semi-variable costs, often referred to as mixed costs, encompass both fixed and variable elements, such as maintenance and utilities tied to production levels.

By understanding these cost categories, you can identify where inefficiencies lie. A careful examination might reveal redundancies, overstaffing, or underutilized assets. Equipped with this knowledge, you can then optimize your operations, streamline processes, and trim excesses.

Implementing Lean Principles for Efficiency

Lean principles, pioneered by Toyota, have transcended the automotive industry to become a cornerstone of efficiency in business operations. At its core, lean thinking centers on eliminating waste—any activity or process that doesn't add value to the end product or service. The goal is to create a streamlined and agile organization that responds to customer needs while minimizing resources spent on non-value-added tasks.

To embark on a lean journey, you must scrutinize every aspect of your business processes. Map out your workflows and identify bottlenecks or areas prone to errors. Implement practices like 5S (Sort, Set in order, Shine, Standardize, Sustain) to organize workspaces and eliminate clutter. Furthermore, embrace continuous improvement through practices like Kaizen, encouraging employees to identify and suggest incremental changes that enhance efficiency.

Negotiating with Suppliers for Favorable Terms
In the intricate web of business, your suppliers play a crucial role in shaping your profitability. Effective supplier negotiations can significantly impact your bottom line. Engaging in strategic negotiations goes beyond simply haggling for lower prices; it's about forging symbiotic relationships that lead to mutually beneficial outcomes.

Preparation is the foundation of successful negotiations. Research your suppliers thoroughly, understand market rates, and assess their financial stability. This equips you with valuable insights that can strengthen your bargaining position. Negotiate not only on price but also on terms— extended payment schedules or bulk purchase discounts can work in your favor.

However, it's important to approach negotiations as a collaborative endeavor rather than a confrontational battle. By building rapport and focusing on shared objectives, you can cultivate long-term partnerships that result in more favorable terms and potentially exclusive arrangements.

Cost control and profit enhancement are not mere buzzwords; they are the bedrock upon which sustainable profitability is built. The strategies outlined in this sub-chapter—identifying and reducing unnecessary costs, implementing lean principles for efficiency, and negotiating with suppliers for favorable terms—offer a blueprint for navigating the complex terrain of financial management. As you navigate this terrain, remember that the pursuit of profitability is a continuous journey, one that demands vigilance, innovation, and a keen understanding of the ever-changing business landscape. By mastering these strategies, you equip yourself with the tools to transform your business into a profit-generating powerhouse in any economic climate.

Capitalizing on Financial Opportunities for Growth

Welcome to the crucial realm of financial management, where the strategic allocation of resources can fuel your business's growth and profitability. In this sub-chapter, we delve into the art and science of capitalizing on financial opportunities for substantial expansion and sustained profit. Prepare to navigate the intricate landscape of funding sources, comprehend the complexities of cost of capital, and master the judicious art of leveraging debt for profit acceleration.

Different Sources of Funding for Business Expansion
Funding forms the bedrock of any business endeavor, especially when aiming for expansion. The key to capitalizing on financial opportunities lies in a diversified approach to funding sources. From traditional avenues to innovative methods, each source carries its unique advantages and considerations.

1. Equity Financing: The cornerstone of business expansion, equity financing involves selling shares of your company to investors. This can infuse fresh capital into your business while spreading the risk among shareholders. However, dilution of ownership and decision-making authority must be weighed against the capital infusion.

2. Debt Financing: Borrowing funds from lenders, such as banks or financial institutions, is a common method for expansion. It allows you to maintain ownership and control, but the obligation to repay the principal along with interest is a critical consideration.

3. Venture Capital and Angel Investors: These investors provide capital to early-stage businesses in exchange for equity. Their expertise and industry connections can be invaluable, but they typically demand a higher return on investment.

4. Crowdfunding: An emerging avenue, crowdfunding allows you to raise capital from a large number of individuals, often in exchange for products, rewards, or future equity. It's an excellent way to gauge market interest while securing funds.

5. Bootstrapping: Sometimes, the best way to fund growth is through your business's own profits. While slower, it ensures you retain full ownership and autonomy.

Calculating the Cost of Capital and Return on Investment
As you consider funding options, it's essential to understand the cost of capital—the rate of return required by investors or lenders. Calculating this involves factoring in the cost of equity, debt, and other financial instruments in the capital structure. A judicious assessment of the cost of capital helps you evaluate the feasibility of potential projects or investments.

Simultaneously, return on investment (ROI) is your compass for measuring the profitability of a venture. To calculate ROI, divide the net profit of an investment by its initial cost and express it as a percentage. Understanding the relationship between ROI and cost of capital provides insights into whether a venture is generating value beyond the capital invested.

Managing Debt and Leveraging for Profit Acceleration
Debt, when managed effectively, can be a potent catalyst for growth. But it requires a prudent balance between risk and reward. Leveraging involves utilizing borrowed funds to magnify returns on investments. It can amplify profits,

but it's a double-edged sword that necessitates a firm grasp of your business's risk tolerance.

When managing debt, consider factors like interest rates, repayment terms, and the purpose of the loan. Leveraging should align with your business's growth strategies and capacity to generate returns that exceed the cost of borrowing. Caution and calculated risk-taking are essential to avoid overleveraging, which could lead to financial instability.

Capitalizing on financial opportunities demands a holistic understanding of funding sources, cost of capital, and leveraging strategies. As you traverse the landscape of financial management, remember that each decision you make influences not only the growth trajectory of your business but also its long-term profitability. By mastering these principles, you wield the power to transform financial resources into sustainable success.

Chapter 6: Innovating Products and Services for Market Dominance

Fostering a Culture of Innovation and Creativity

In the dynamic landscape of business, where markets evolve at a rapid pace, fostering a culture of innovation and creativity has become more crucial than ever. This sub chapter delves into the foundational principles and strategies that lay the groundwork for cultivating an environment in which innovation thrives, enabling businesses to create products and services that not only meet the needs of today's consumers but also shape the demands of tomorrow.

Creating an Environment that Encourages Innovation

At the heart of innovation lies an environment that encourages free thinking, idea sharing, and the fearless pursuit of novel solutions. Forward-thinking organizations understand that innovation cannot be coerced but rather emerges naturally when employees feel empowered and valued. To create such an environment, leaders must communicate a clear message that innovation is not only allowed but also actively encouraged.

Open communication channels play a pivotal role in nurturing innovation. Regular brainstorming sessions, innovation workshops, and cross-functional collaboration foster a sense of shared purpose among employees. Moreover, leaders must demonstrate a willingness to listen to diverse perspectives and be open to unconventional ideas. By cultivating an inclusive environment where everyone's input is valued, businesses lay the foundation for groundbreaking innovations.

Empowering Employees to Contribute Innovative Ideas
Innovation is not the sole purview of a select few; rather, it should be a collective effort involving every member of the organization. Empowering employees to contribute innovative ideas requires creating a sense of ownership and trust. When individuals feel that their contributions are respected and taken seriously, they become more invested in the organization's success.

One effective approach is establishing innovation forums or digital platforms where employees can share their ideas openly. These platforms facilitate idea exchange across hierarchies, ensuring that creativity is not stifled by traditional organizational structures. Encouraging employees to dedicate a portion of their time to working on self-directed projects or "innovation time" is another strategy that Google and other successful companies have employed to great effect. This practice allows employees to pursue ideas outside their immediate job roles, sparking innovative thinking across departments.

Balancing Risk-Taking with Calculated Experimentation
Innovation inherently involves a degree of risk-taking. Yet, the key to successful innovation is not reckless abandon but rather calculated experimentation. Leaders must strike a

delicate balance between encouraging audacious thinking and providing a safety net for potential failures.

A culture that embraces failure as a stepping stone to success is a hallmark of organizations that drive innovation. When employees are not penalized for failures but rather encouraged to learn from them, they become more willing to take risks and explore uncharted territories. This culture of experimentation can lead to breakthroughs that transform the business landscape.

One way to manage risk is through incremental innovation. Instead of aiming for monumental leaps, businesses can focus on making small, iterative improvements to existing products and processes. This approach minimizes potential losses while gradually pushing the boundaries of innovation. Additionally, investing in robust feedback mechanisms and prototype testing allows organizations to identify flaws early in the development process, reducing the risk of costly failures down the line.

Fostering a culture of innovation and creativity is not a one-size-fits-all endeavor. It requires a strategic commitment from leadership, a willingness to challenge traditional norms, and a steadfast belief in the potential of every employee to contribute to the innovation journey. By creating an environment that encourages innovation, empowering employees to think beyond the conventional, and balancing risk-taking with calculated experimentation, businesses can position themselves at the forefront of their industries, ready to shape the future with transformative products and services. As we move forward, the organizations that prioritize innovation will not only survive but also thrive in the ever-evolving landscape of business.

The Art of Product/Service Development and Enhancement

In the fast-paced world of business, the ability to innovate and adapt is often the key that separates market leaders from the rest. When it comes to maintaining a competitive edge, constant enhancement of products and services is an indispensable strategy. In this sub chapter, we'll delve into the art of product and service development and enhancement, exploring the critical steps and strategies to not only meet customer needs but to exceed them.

Identifying Customer Pain Points and Needs

At the heart of successful product and service innovation lies a deep understanding of your customers. By pinpointing their pain points and needs, you uncover opportunities to provide solutions that resonate profoundly. Market research, surveys, and direct engagement can provide valuable insights into what your customers truly desire.

Imagine a business that offers a mobile app for task management. Through careful research, they discover that users struggle with overwhelming to-do lists and task prioritization. This insight allows them to design features that aid in task organization, remind users of important deadlines, and enhance overall productivity.

Iterative Design and Continuous Improvement
Gone are the days of static products that remain unchanged for years. Iterative design, an approach focused on incremental improvements, is the cornerstone of modern product development. This process involves creating a prototype, testing it in the real world, collecting feedback, and then refining the product based on that feedback. By continuously refining and enhancing, businesses can create products that stay aligned with evolving customer needs.

Consider a smartphone manufacturer that releases annual updates to its flagship model. With each iteration, they address user feedback, fine-tune features, and introduce new technologies. This iterative approach not only maintains customer loyalty but also attracts new customers looking for the latest innovations.

Implementing Customer Feedback for Innovation
The most valuable insights often come directly from the customers who use your products and services. Implementing a system for collecting, analyzing, and acting upon customer feedback is crucial for innovation. Whether through surveys, online reviews, or focus groups, this

feedback offers a wealth of information to guide enhancements.

Picture an online retail platform that encourages users to review their purchases. By meticulously analyzing these reviews, the platform identifies common complaints about shipping delays. In response, they streamline their logistics processes, leading to faster delivery times and increased customer satisfaction.

Innovation driven by customer feedback doesn't just stop at solving existing problems; it can also reveal unmet needs. By listening closely to your customers, you can identify opportunities to introduce entirely new features or services that they didn't even realize they needed.

The art of product and service development and enhancement is an ongoing journey that requires a deep connection with your customers and a commitment to constant improvement. By understanding customer pain points, embracing iterative design, and actively implementing customer feedback, businesses can position themselves as leaders in their industries. Remember, in today's dynamic market, innovation isn't a luxury—it's a necessity for long-term success and market dominance.

Patenting and Protecting Your Innovative Ideas

In the dynamic landscape of modern business, where innovation is the driving force behind market success, protecting your groundbreaking ideas is akin to fortifying the foundation of your empire. This subchapter is a voyage into the world of intellectual property, a realm where the magic of creativity meets the meticulous art of legal protection. Embark on this journey as we explore the intricacies of patenting, unravel the threads of intellectual property rights, and unveil the strategies to wield patents as your weapons of competitive advantage.

Navigating the Patenting Process Effectively

Imagine crafting an invention that promises to reshape industries and captivate consumer imagination. Now, envision that same invention becoming a target for imitation or exploitation. This is where the patenting process emerges as the guardian of innovation, a legal mechanism that grants exclusive rights to your creation. However, the path to securing a patent is complex and multifaceted, demanding a profound understanding of the process.

1. Invention Assessment: Before embarking on the journey of patenting, it's crucial to conduct a thorough assessment of your invention. Is it truly unique, offering something that no one else has thought of? Does it have a real-world application that brings value to users?

2. Patent Search: The patenting process begins with a diligent search to ensure that your invention hasn't already been patented by another entity. This search extends beyond domestic boundaries, covering international patents as well.

3. Patent Application: Crafting a compelling patent application is an art in itself. The document must intricately describe your invention, its technical details, and its potential applications. Clarity, precision, and attention to detail are paramount in the writing process.

4. Legal Expertise: Engaging a patent attorney is not merely a recommendation but a necessity. These legal experts specialize in guiding you through the complexities of the patenting process, ensuring that your application adheres to legal standards and effectively protects your invention.

5. Patent Office Review: Upon submitting your application, it undergoes a meticulous examination by patent office professionals. Be prepared for potential rejections or requests for modifications. Patience and resilience are vital during this phase.

Safeguarding Intellectual Property from Infringement
Securing a patent is the first step in protecting your intellectual property; the next is guarding it against potential infringers. Intellectual property infringement can undermine the fruits of your labor and devalue your innovation. Thus, a proactive approach to enforcement is essential.

1. Competitor Monitoring: Keep a vigilant eye on the activities of competitors, both old and new. Regularly review their products, services, and marketing materials to ensure they are not benefiting from your patented ideas.

2. Cease and Desist: If you suspect infringement, your patent attorney can assist in sending a cease-and-desist letter to the alleged infringing party. This formal communication puts them on notice and often initiates discussions to resolve the matter amicably.

3. Legal Action: While litigation is not the preferred route, it can be necessary to protect your rights. Engaging in legal action sends a clear message that you are willing to defend your intellectual property.

Leveraging Patents for Competitive Advantage and Profit
Patents are not just legal shields; they are strategic tools that can be wielded to carve a path of success in the market. Leveraging patents can bring about significant benefits to your business.

1. Licensing and Partnerships: Your patented technology can become a revenue generator through licensing. By permitting others to use your innovation for a fee, you not only expand your income streams but also broaden the reach of your ideas.

2. Market Differentiation: In a sea of competitors, a patent distinguishes your products and services as innovative and unique. This differentiation can attract customers seeking cutting-edge solutions.

3. Negotiation Power: Holding a patent elevates your negotiating power in collaborations and partnerships. It becomes a bargaining chip that can lead to mutually beneficial agreements.

4. Monetization: Beyond licensing, you can monetize your patents by selling them outright. Companies that recognize the value of your technology might be interested in acquiring your intellectual property.

The journey of patenting and protecting your innovative ideas is a strategic endeavor that requires careful planning, legal acumen, and unwavering vigilance. When navigated skillfully, patents can serve as both shields and swords – protecting your creations and empowering you to conquer markets. By understanding the nuances of the patenting process, vigilantly guarding against infringement, and tactically leveraging patents for profit, you transform your innovative ideas into formidable assets that drive your business toward market dominance and lasting success.

Chapter 7: Sales Strategies for Profit Amplification

Developing a High-Performing Sales Team

In the dynamic world of business, where profitability is the ultimate goal, the sales team stands as the frontline warriors driving revenue and growth. Developing a high-performing sales team isn't just about finding individuals who can sell; it's about cultivating a dynamic force that understands your company's vision, products, and customer needs, and can translate those insights into tangible results. In this sub-chapter, we will delve deep into the art of recruiting and training effective sales professionals, setting clear sales targets and performance metrics, and mastering the art of motivating and incentivizing your sales team for optimal outcomes.

Recruiting and Training Effective Sales Professionals

Recruiting top-tier sales professionals is a cornerstone of building a high-performing sales team. It's not just about seeking individuals with impressive track records, but also about finding candidates who resonate with your company culture and values. While experience is crucial, a genuine enthusiasm for your products or services can set a candidate apart. Look for candidates who possess strong communication skills, empathy, and a keen ability to listen and understand customer pain points.

Once the right candidates are identified, an intensive and well-structured training program becomes indispensable.

Sales training should encompass not only product knowledge but also techniques for effective communication, objection handling, and relationship building. A successful salesperson not only understands what they're selling but also knows how to address customer concerns and provide tailored solutions. Ongoing training, workshops, and mentorship opportunities are equally important to keep the team updated with market trends and evolving customer expectations.

Setting Clear Sales Targets and Performance Metrics
Sales without targets are like ships without a destination. Clear and achievable sales targets provide the roadmap for the team's efforts. These targets should be specific, measurable, attainable, relevant, and time-bound (SMART). By breaking down larger revenue goals into smaller, actionable targets, the team gains a sense of direction and purpose.

Performance metrics are the guiding stars that help monitor progress towards those targets. Metrics such as sales revenue, conversion rates, average deal size, and sales cycle duration provide valuable insights into the team's performance. Regular analysis of these metrics enables proactive identification of bottlenecks and opportunities, allowing adjustments to strategies as needed.

Motivating and Incentivizing the Sales Team for Results
Even the most skilled sales professionals can experience burnout without proper motivation and incentives. While financial incentives like commissions and bonuses play a significant role, intrinsic motivators are equally crucial. Recognition, appreciation, and opportunities for growth can fuel a salesperson's passion and commitment.

Effective leadership is pivotal in motivating the team. A great leader understands individual strengths and weaknesses, provides constructive feedback, and offers a supportive environment that encourages learning and innovation. Regular team meetings, brainstorming sessions, and open communication channels foster camaraderie and keep the team aligned with overarching goals.

Developing a high-performing sales team is an investment that pays exponential dividends. Recruiting individuals who resonate with your company's mission, training them extensively, setting clear targets and performance metrics, and fostering a motivating environment collectively create a powerhouse of revenue generation. Remember, a successful sales team isn't just about closing deals; it's about building lasting relationships, understanding customer needs, and driving sustainable profitability.

The journey to creating such a team isn't without its challenges, but with the right strategies and commitment, you can elevate your sales force to achieve remarkable outcomes. As you embark on this path, keep in mind that the journey is ongoing, requiring continuous refinement, innovation, and adaptability. Your sales team isn't just a revenue generator; it's a reflection of your business's values, dedication, and pursuit of excellence. With the right approach, you can mold your sales team into a force that not only drives profits but also leaves a lasting positive impact on your company's success.

Remember, it's the synergy of recruiting, training, setting targets, and nurturing motivation that creates the foundation for a sales team that consistently achieves and surpasses its goals. The Midas Touch Secret in sales lies not in turning everything to gold, but in transforming dedicated professionals into gold-standard revenue generators.

Implementing Consultative Selling Techniques
In the dynamic landscape of modern business, where customers are increasingly informed and discerning, traditional sales approaches are losing their effectiveness. Enter consultative selling, a strategic approach that is rapidly gaining ground due to its customer-centric nature and proven success in driving profits. This sub chapter will delve deep into the art and science of consultative selling techniques, equipping you with the insights needed to amplify your sales and enhance your business's profitability.

Understanding the Customer's Pain Points and Needs
Consultative selling is built upon a fundamental truth:
customers don't just buy products or services; they seek
solutions to their problems and desires. Understanding
these pain points and needs is the cornerstone of effective
consultative selling.

At its core, this technique demands that you truly listen to
your customers. Not merely with the intent to respond, but
with the intent to comprehend. By asking probing questions
and actively listening to their responses, you gain a clear
understanding of their challenges, aspirations, and
expectations. This knowledge empowers you to tailor your
offerings to precisely match their needs, making the sales
process more relevant and engaging.

Building Trust and Rapport through Consultative Selling
In a marketplace where skepticism often reigns, trust is a
rare and invaluable currency. Consultative selling, by its
very nature, fosters trust and rapport between the
salesperson and the customer. How? By shifting the focus
from the sale to the relationship.

Rather than pushing products, consultative sellers act as
advisors. They establish themselves as experts in their field,
capable of guiding customers towards the best possible
solution. This transformational shift allows for the building
of genuine relationships based on trust and credibility.
When customers perceive you as a partner invested in their
success, the likelihood of repeat business and referrals
skyrockets.

Overcoming Objections and Closing Deals Effectively
The path from identifying a customer's needs to sealing the deal is seldom without hurdles. Objections, whether related to cost, features, or concerns, are a natural part of the sales process. This is where consultative selling shines. It equips you with the tools needed to address objections intelligently and convert them into opportunities.

When you've taken the time to understand the customer's pain points, objections become openings for dialogue rather than roadblocks. By acknowledging their concerns empathetically and offering tailored solutions, you demonstrate your commitment to their satisfaction. This personalized approach minimizes resistance and paves the way for a smoother closing process.

The art of closing deals effectively in consultative selling hinges on your ability to provide a solution that addresses the customer's unique needs. By effectively linking the benefits of your product or service to the resolution of their challenges, you create a compelling case for making the purchase. This approach not only increases the likelihood of a successful transaction but also fosters long-term customer loyalty.

Consultative selling is not a fleeting trend; it's a fundamental shift in the way sales are conducted. It aligns seamlessly with today's customer expectations, placing their needs at the forefront. By understanding their pain points, building trust, and adeptly addressing objections, you position yourself not just as a seller, but as a valuable ally on their journey. Through these techniques, your sales efforts will not only drive profits but also establish your brand as a trusted partner in the marketplace.

As you embark on your journey into consultative selling, remember that it requires a genuine commitment to understanding and serving your customers. This isn't about using scripted tactics; it's about developing meaningful relationships and making a positive impact. The rewards, both in terms of increased profits and a stronger brand reputation, will undoubtedly be worth the effort.

Utilizing Technology for Sales Optimization

In the ever-evolving landscape of business, where customer preferences and market trends shift rapidly, one truth remains constant: the art of selling is the cornerstone of profitability. Sales strategies form the nucleus of any successful business endeavor, and in today's digital age, technology has emerged as a potent catalyst for optimizing these strategies. In this sub-chapter, we will delve into the intricate world of technology-driven sales optimization, exploring how integrating Customer Relationship Management (CRM) systems, automating sales processes, and analyzing sales data can pave the way for strategic decision-making and unprecedented profit growth.

Integrating CRM Systems for Customer Insights

In the digital age, customers demand personalization and exceptional service. This is where CRM systems come into play. A CRM system serves as the hub of customer information, allowing businesses to cultivate deep and meaningful relationships. By consolidating data from various touchpoints, including interactions on social media, website visits, and purchase history, businesses can gain comprehensive insights into customer behaviors, preferences, and pain points. This wealth of information enables sales teams to tailor their approach, creating targeted pitches that resonate with individual customers.

Moreover, CRM systems empower businesses to track customer interactions seamlessly. This not only enhances communication and accountability within the team but also ensures that no lead or inquiry falls through the cracks. In essence, CRM integration transforms the sales process from transactional to relational, elevating customer experiences and boosting the likelihood of repeat business and referrals.

Automating Sales Processes for Efficiency

Time, they say, is money. In the realm of sales, this adage takes on even greater significance. Automating sales processes not only accelerates the pace at which deals are closed but also ensures consistency in approach. Repetitive tasks, such as sending follow-up emails, generating invoices, and updating lead status, can be automated, liberating sales professionals from administrative burdens. This, in turn, allows them to focus on what truly matters: building relationships and closing deals.

Automated workflows, triggered by specific actions or milestones, streamline the sales journey. For instance, when a lead reaches a certain engagement level, an automated email containing targeted content can be sent, nurturing the lead further down the sales funnel. By engaging prospects with relevant information at the right time, businesses can increase conversion rates and accelerate the sales cycle.

Analyzing Sales Data for Strategic Decision-Making
In the digital age, data is a treasure trove waiting to be unlocked. By harnessing the power of analytics, businesses can transform raw data into actionable insights. Sales data, in particular, provides a roadmap to understanding customer behavior, market trends, and the efficacy of sales strategies.

Sophisticated analytics tools can unveil patterns in purchasing behavior, shedding light on which products or services are in demand and when. This insight informs inventory management, ensuring that businesses are well-prepared to meet customer needs. Additionally, data-driven sales forecasting enables companies to project future revenues accurately, aiding in budgeting and resource allocation.

Beyond predictive analysis, data can also spotlight underperforming areas of the sales process. By identifying bottlenecks or drop-off points in the funnel, businesses can refine their approach and optimize conversion rates. This iterative process of refinement, based on data insights, is a hallmark of successful sales strategies.

The digital revolution has reshaped the landscape of sales strategies. Integrating CRM systems, automating sales processes, and analyzing sales data can amplify profit margins and fortify customer relationships. As businesses continue to navigate the complex intersection of technology and sales, those who master the art of leveraging these tools stand poised to unlock new dimensions of profitability and success. Stay ahead of the curve, adapt to technological advancements, and watch as your sales strategies become the Midas Touch in your pursuit of profitability.

Chapter 8: Customer Relationship Management and Retention

Creating Exceptional Customer Experiences

In the rapidly evolving landscape of business, where products and services can be replicated and imitated, the true differentiator that sets a company apart lies in the realm of customer experiences. Crafting exceptional customer experiences is not just a buzzword; it is the cornerstone of a business's profitability and long-term success. As we delve into the heart of this sub-chapter, we will explore the profound significance of customer-centricity in driving profitability, the art of personalizing interactions for heightened engagement, and the strategic prowess required to effectively address and resolve customer issues and complaints.

Importance of Customer-Centricity in Profitability

In a business environment that constantly adapts to changing customer preferences, understanding and prioritizing customer needs is paramount. Every interaction, transaction, and touch point forms a part of the customer journey, which shapes their perception of your brand. Customer-centricity is not just about providing good service; it's about creating an emotional connection that fosters loyalty and advocacy. This connection is not a one-time occurrence, but a continuous process that translates into repeat business, increased spending, and positive word-of-mouth marketing.

Companies that genuinely put their customers at the center of their operations are better equipped to adapt to market shifts, as they have an intricate understanding of their audience's desires and pain points. Such businesses don't just react; they proactively anticipate their customers' needs and innovate accordingly. This philosophy isn't limited to any particular industry; it extends from retail and hospitality to B2B enterprises, where forging strong relationships can lead to long-term contracts and mutual growth.

Personalizing Interactions for Enhanced Engagement
Gone are the days when generic messages and one-size-fits-all marketing strategies were sufficient. Modern consumers expect tailored experiences that resonate with their individual preferences and needs. Personalization doesn't just mean addressing customers by their names; it involves understanding their preferences, purchase history, and behaviors to provide customized solutions.

To achieve this level of personalization, businesses are turning to data analytics and artificial intelligence. By analyzing vast amounts of data, companies can gain insights into customers' buying patterns, interests, and behaviors. These insights allow businesses to segment their customer base and deliver targeted messages, recommendations, and offers that are not only relevant but also enhance the overall experience. Personalization goes beyond marketing; it extends to product recommendations, website interfaces, and even after-sales support.

Resolving Customer Issues and Complaints Effectively
Every business, no matter how well it operates, will encounter customer issues and complaints. However, the way these issues are handled can make or break a customer's loyalty. Swift and effective resolution showcases your commitment to customer satisfaction and can even turn a dissatisfied customer into a loyal advocate.

Creating a seamless process for resolving issues involves not only well-trained customer service representatives but also robust systems for tracking and managing complaints. Businesses can use technology to their advantage by implementing customer relationship management (CRM) software that centralizes customer information and interactions. This empowers customer service teams to address issues more efficiently, access historical data, and personalize solutions based on the customer's history.

The key to resolving issues lies in active listening and empathy. When customers feel heard and understood, they are more likely to remain loyal. Moreover, businesses can turn these challenges into opportunities for improvement. Analyzing the root causes of complaints can lead to process enhancements that prevent similar issues from arising in the future.

Creating exceptional customer experiences isn't just a matter of courtesy; it's a strategic imperative that drives profitability and long-term success. Businesses that prioritize customer-centricity, personalize interactions, and handle issues effectively stand to gain not only increased revenue but also the intangible benefits of strong customer loyalty, brand advocacy, and market resilience. As you embark on this journey of crafting remarkable customer experiences, remember that each interaction is an opportunity to make a lasting impact and turn your customers into not just buyers, but passionate brand advocates.

Building Customer Loyalty and Advocacy

In the ever-evolving landscape of business, where competition is fierce and consumer choices are abundant, one key factor remains constant: the value of customer loyalty. In this sub-chapter, we delve into the art of cultivating customer loyalty and transforming satisfied buyers into brand advocates who not only stick around but also actively promote your business to others. We will explore the strategic implementation of loyalty programs, the art of encouraging customer referrals and testimonials, and the delicate task of nurturing enduring customer relationships.

Developing Loyalty Programs and Rewards

Loyalty programs are akin to a nurturing embrace for your customers—a gesture that conveys your appreciation for their consistent patronage. Such programs not only keep your clientele engaged but also provide them with a tangible reason to return. A well-designed loyalty program goes beyond the rudimentary "buy more, get more" approach. It should reflect your brand's values, resonate with your customers' desires, and provide a seamless experience.

Consider Starbucks, an emblematic example of an effective loyalty program. The Starbucks Rewards program offers a tiered system that grants customers stars for every purchase. These stars accumulate and unlock various benefits, from free drinks to personalized offers. The brilliance of this strategy lies in its simplicity and the perception of value it provides to customers. When contemplating your loyalty program, focus on what your customers truly value, whether it's exclusive access, discounts, or personalized experiences.

Encouraging Customer Referrals and Testimonials
Word-of-mouth has long been hailed as one of the most potent marketing tools, and for good reason. Satisfied customers have the power to become your most fervent promoters, provided you provide them with the incentive to do so. Encouraging customer referrals can be as simple as offering a referral bonus or discount for both the referring customer and the referred one. Dropbox's referral program is an iconic case in point—it offered free additional storage to both the referrer and the referred, resulting in a significant boost in sign-ups.

Furthermore, testimonials wield considerable influence over prospective customers. People tend to trust the experiences of their peers more than any marketing campaign. Reach out to your satisfied customers and request honest feedback in the form of testimonials. Showcase these testimonials on your website, social media, and marketing materials. Video testimonials can be particularly impactful, as they provide an authentic and relatable touch.

Monitoring and Nurturing Long-Term Customer Relationships

As the saying goes, "Rome wasn't built in a day." Similarly, nurturing long-term customer relationships requires consistent effort and genuine care. It's not enough to win over a customer; you must work to keep them engaged and satisfied over time. Regular communication is key—send personalized messages on special occasions, offer exclusive discounts, and keep them informed about new products or updates.

Moreover, the digital age has endowed businesses with an array of tools for monitoring and enhancing customer relationships. Customer relationship management (CRM) software allows you to track interactions, preferences, and purchase history. Leverage this data to tailor your communications and offerings. Remember, the goal is to foster a sense of belonging and importance, making your customers feel valued beyond their transactions.

Building customer loyalty and advocacy isn't a mere transactional pursuit; it's an investment in the sustainability and growth of your business. By developing innovative loyalty programs, harnessing the power of referrals and testimonials, and maintaining genuine, long-term relationships, you can create a community of loyal customers who not only contribute to your bottom line but also serve as ambassadors for your brand. Remember, in the world of business, loyalty truly is the golden ticket to sustained success.

Customer Feedback and Continuous Improvement

In the fast-paced world of business, where customer preferences and market trends are in constant flux, maintaining a competitive edge requires more than just a stellar product or service. It demands an unwavering commitment to understanding your customers' needs, exceeding their expectations, and continuously fine-tuning your offerings. This is where the strategic use of customer feedback and the pursuit of continuous improvement come into play. In this sub-chapter, we'll delve into the art of gathering valuable customer feedback, harnessing it to enhance your products and services, and fostering transparent communication that reinforces customer loyalty.

Gathering Feedback through Surveys and Reviews
The foundation of any successful customer feedback strategy is rooted in proactive outreach. Surveys and reviews serve as powerful tools to gain insight into customer experiences and perceptions. By crafting thoughtfully designed surveys, you can obtain quantifiable data that sheds light on various aspects of your business, from product quality to customer service efficiency. These surveys should be concise, relevant, and tailored to elicit actionable responses.

When creating surveys, consider utilizing a mix of closed-ended questions with rating scales and open-ended questions that encourage customers to express themselves freely. Closed-ended questions provide valuable quantitative data, while open-ended questions offer qualitative insights that can uncover nuanced opinions and suggestions.

Similarly, online reviews have become a crucial touchpoint for customers to voice their opinions. Encourage customers to leave reviews on platforms relevant to your industry. Monitor these reviews closely, responding promptly to both positive and negative feedback. The latter presents a valuable opportunity for service recovery and demonstrates your commitment to customer satisfaction.

Using Feedback to Enhance Products and Services
Feedback gathered from surveys and reviews serves as a goldmine of actionable information. Analyzing this feedback requires a systematic approach to categorize,

prioritize, and address the issues raised by customers. Remember, the goal is not just to fix existing problems, but to anticipate and prevent future ones.

Pay attention to recurring themes in feedback. Are customers consistently highlighting a particular pain point or suggesting improvements? Use this data to fuel your product development process. Implementing changes based on customer feedback not only enhances customer satisfaction but also demonstrates that you value their opinions.

As you iterate your products or services based on feedback, communicate these improvements to your customer base. Highlight how their input has directly contributed to positive changes. This not only shows that you're actively listening but also fosters a sense of partnership between your business and its customers.

Communicating Improvements to Customers for Transparency
Transparency is a cornerstone of customer-centric businesses. When you implement changes based on customer feedback, share this information openly and transparently. Craft targeted communications to inform customers about enhancements and improvements.

Consider using multiple communication channels, such as email newsletters, social media, and website updates. Provide insights into the specific changes you've made, how they address customer concerns, and the benefits customers can expect to experience.

Transparency extends beyond just communicating improvements. If certain suggestions from customers aren't feasible due to technical constraints or other reasons, explain the rationale behind your decisions. Customers appreciate honesty and clarity, even when their suggestions can't be implemented.

Customer feedback is a potent tool that, when wielded strategically, can transform your business into a customer-centric powerhouse. By actively seeking input through surveys and reviews, harnessing that feedback for product and service enhancements, and transparently communicating those changes, you create a cycle of continuous improvement that not only keeps your customers satisfied but also fuels your business growth.

Chapter 9: Adapting to Market Changes and Trends

Embracing Business Agility for Profitable Resilience

In the dynamic landscape of business, change is the only constant. In a world driven by evolving customer preferences, technological advancements, and economic fluctuations, the ability to adapt swiftly is no longer a luxury – it's a necessity. This sub-chapter delves into the critical concept of embracing business agility as a cornerstone of profitable resilience.

Recognizing the Importance of Adaptability

The winds of change can be unpredictable and even disruptive. Businesses that fail to recognize and adapt to these changes risk being left behind, unable to meet evolving customer demands or effectively compete. Recognizing the importance of adaptability means acknowledging that the strategies and practices that brought success in the past might not guarantee success in the future.

In the context of profitability, adaptability ensures that an enterprise remains relevant, even when market conditions shift dramatically. It enables companies to stay ahead of the curve by anticipating changes and adjusting their operations, products, and services accordingly. The first step toward profitable resilience is cultivating a mindset that embraces change not as a threat but as an opportunity for growth.

Agile Methodologies for Quick Response to Change

Agile methodologies, long heralded in software development, have now become a staple for businesses across various sectors. The core principle of agility involves breaking down large, complex tasks into smaller, manageable components. This approach allows for quicker iterations, enabling businesses to respond rapidly to changing circumstances.

Agile methodologies are characterized by their iterative and incremental approach. Instead of rigid long-term plans, businesses using agile methods prioritize flexibility. This means that when a new trend emerges or customer preferences shift, the business can adjust its strategies without needing to overhaul its entire operation.

The Agile Manifesto, with its emphasis on individuals and interactions, working solutions, and customer collaboration, provides a blueprint for businesses to stay nimble in a rapidly evolving landscape. Agile frameworks like Scrum and Kanban offer structured processes that enable teams to deliver value incrementally, adapt to feedback, and pivot as needed.

Pivoting Strategies Without Compromising Profitability

Pivoting is the strategic art of changing direction while preserving your core business objectives. It's about making calculated shifts in response to emerging trends, disruptive technologies, or unforeseen challenges. Successful businesses pivot not out of panic but out of a deep understanding of their market, a willingness to learn, and an unwavering commitment to profitability.

To pivot effectively, a business must begin by thoroughly assessing the market landscape and its own strengths and weaknesses. This evaluation provides the foundation for identifying the areas where change is needed and determining the best way to implement that change. The key to successful pivoting is to avoid compromising profitability during the transition.

Pivoting strategies should be guided by the principle of maintaining a strong value proposition. While adapting to new trends or technologies, businesses must ensure that they continue to meet customer needs effectively. This requires clear communication with customers, transparency about changes, and a focus on delivering value throughout the transition.

Embracing business agility is more than just a buzzword; it's a strategic imperative. The ability to adapt swiftly and effectively to market changes and trends is what separates thriving businesses from those that falter. By recognizing the importance of adaptability, employing agile methodologies, and pivoting strategies without compromising profitability, businesses can position themselves for long-term success in an ever-evolving world. Remember, the path to profitable resilience begins with a mindset that welcomes change as an opportunity and not a challenge.

Capitalizing on Emerging Industry Trends

In the ever-evolving landscape of business, staying ahead of the curve is not just a strategy; it's a necessity. The ability to adapt to emerging industry trends can mean the difference between thriving and merely surviving in a competitive marketplace. As we delve into this sub chapter, we'll explore the art of capitalizing on emerging trends, highlighting the importance of staying informed, seizing opportunities, and maintaining a delicate balance between innovation and core business stability.

Staying Informed about Industry Developments

In the dynamic world of business, industry trends can emerge seemingly overnight, reshaping entire sectors and leaving unprepared businesses in the dust. To effectively capitalize on emerging trends, businesses must first establish a robust system for staying informed. This entails proactive research, continuous market analysis, and establishing connections with thought leaders and industry experts. Regularly monitoring trade publications, attending industry conferences, and participating in networking events can provide invaluable insights that serve as early indicators of potential trends.

Digital technologies, like social media and online forums, have drastically enhanced our ability to access real-time information. Engaging in online industry communities and following influential voices on platforms like LinkedIn or Twitter can help you gauge shifting sentiments and anticipate forthcoming shifts in consumer behavior. Additionally, consider investing in data analysis tools that allow you to track market patterns and customer preferences, enabling you to react swiftly to emerging trends.

Seizing Opportunities Presented by New Trends
Identifying an emerging trend is one thing; effectively capitalizing on it is an art that requires strategic finesse. The key is to recognize not only the trend itself but also the underlying opportunities it presents. When a trend gains momentum, it's often accompanied by a set of consumer needs that are not yet being met by existing solutions. Entrepreneurs who can swiftly design products or services that cater to these needs stand to gain a significant competitive advantage.

Consider the meteoric rise of mobile applications. As smartphones became ubiquitous, businesses that recognized the trend and developed apps to enhance user experiences reaped substantial rewards. The trend wasn't just about the smartphones themselves; it was about the new ways people were interacting with technology. By identifying this shift and creating innovative solutions, companies like Uber and Airbnb transformed industries and achieved explosive growth.

Balancing Innovation with Core Business Stability
While the allure of chasing every new trend is strong, successful businesses understand the importance of maintaining a stable core even as they innovate. Striking the right balance between innovation and stability is a delicate act that requires astute management. Some trends may align naturally with your business's core competencies, allowing for seamless integration. Others might require more significant shifts in your operations or offerings.

The goal is to avoid chasing trends recklessly, potentially diluting your brand or stretching resources too thin. Instead, approach new trends with a discerning eye. Evaluate how well a trend aligns with your business's mission and values. Does it complement your existing products or services, or does it threaten to divert resources from your core strengths? Remember that not all trends will be relevant or sustainable for your business in the long term.

One successful strategy is to create innovation teams or departments tasked with exploring new trends and opportunities while the core business remains steady. This approach enables you to explore without jeopardizing your established operations. If a trend gains traction and aligns with your core values, you can then integrate it more fully into your business model.

Capitalizing on emerging industry trends is a multifaceted endeavor that demands vigilance, strategic thinking, and a commitment to maintaining your core business stability.

Staying informed about industry developments provides the foundation for seizing opportunities presented by new trends. However, remember that not every trend is a gold mine; each must be evaluated against your business's values and capabilities. By striking the right balance between innovation and stability, you can position your business to thrive in an ever-changing landscape, ensuring that you are not just a follower of trends, but a true industry leader.

Navigating Economic Challenges for Profit Protection

In the fast-paced world of business, one of the most inevitable challenges entrepreneurs and organizations face is economic volatility. Economic downturns, characterized by recessions and financial crises, can significantly impact profitability and sustainability. Navigating these challenges requires a strategic approach that encompasses resilience, flexibility, and forward-thinking. In this sub-chapter, we delve into the art of managing economic turbulence to protect and even enhance your profits.

Strategies for Managing Economic Downturns

Economic downturns, often accompanied by reduced consumer spending and tighter credit markets, demand a proactive approach. One of the fundamental strategies to consider is conserving cash. Liquidity becomes paramount during uncertain times, enabling you to weather the storm and invest opportunistically when the market rebounds. This may involve renegotiating payment terms with suppliers, optimizing inventory levels, and delaying non-essential capital expenditures.

Moreover, diversifying your customer base is a strategic maneuver. Relying heavily on a single market or client can expose your business to heightened risk during economic downturns. By targeting a broader range of industries or geographical locations, you can mitigate the impact of a downturn in any one area.

Cost-Cutting Measures Without Sacrificing Quality
Cost-cutting during economic challenges is a delicate balancing act. While it's crucial to trim unnecessary expenses, it's equally essential to uphold the quality that defines your brand. Begin by scrutinizing your operations for areas of inefficiency. Streamlining processes and eliminating waste can drive significant cost savings without compromising quality.

Furthermore, consider a zero-based budgeting approach. Rather than basing your budget on the previous year's numbers, start from scratch, justifying every expense anew. This method encourages a critical assessment of each line item, facilitating the identification of areas where costs can be reduced.

Diversifying Revenue Streams for Risk Mitigation
Overreliance on a single revenue stream can spell disaster during economic downturns. To shield your profits from the impact of market fluctuations, diversify your sources of revenue. This can involve introducing complementary products or services that cater to your existing customer base.

Moreover, exploring new markets or industries can provide a buffer against economic challenges. This diversification strategy not only reduces risk but also opens up new avenues for growth. Careful market research and due diligence are essential when embarking on these ventures.

Adapting Mindset and Execution
Navigating economic challenges isn't solely about reacting to the external environment; it's also about cultivating the right mindset within your organization. Foster a culture of adaptability and resilience, encouraging your team to remain agile in the face of uncertainty. Promote open communication and collaboration, ensuring that everyone is aligned with the strategies in place.

Furthermore, maintaining a strong relationship with financial institutions can prove invaluable. Establishing trust and open dialogue with banks and lenders can provide access to additional resources during challenging times, helping to keep your operations afloat.

In the intricate dance of business, economic challenges are an inevitable partner. However, armed with the right strategies, you can not only shield your profits but also emerge stronger and more resilient. By managing economic downturns with strategic cash management, judicious cost-cutting, and diversified revenue streams, you position your business to withstand the storms and capitalize on the eventual upturn. Remember, the ability to adapt and thrive during economic challenges is a hallmark of a truly profitable enterprise.

Chapter 10: Effective Leadership and Team Management

Cultivating Leadership Skills for Profitable Guidance

As businesses strive for profitability, effective leadership becomes a cornerstone of success. A skilled leader possesses the Midas touch – the ability to transform their team and business operations into a profitable endeavor. In this sub-chapter, we delve into the traits that distinguish exceptional leaders, the power of leading by example, and the art of nurturing a culture of accountability and empowerment.

Traits of Effective Leaders in Business

Effective leadership isn't just about issuing orders or holding a title; it's about inspiring and guiding a team towards shared objectives. Visionary leaders possess a clear understanding of their business goals and can articulate their vision to the team. This clarity fosters alignment and empowers every team member to contribute effectively.

Furthermore, adaptability is a defining trait. In today's dynamic business landscape, change is constant. Effective leaders navigate uncertainties with resilience, adjusting strategies and plans while maintaining the bigger picture. They are proactive learners, seeking continuous improvement and staying updated on industry trends.

Empathy is another trait that sets exceptional leaders apart. The ability to understand and connect with team members fosters trust and collaboration. Empathetic leaders recognize that every individual brings unique strengths and challenges to the table, and they tailor their guidance accordingly.

Leading by Example and Setting the Tone
Effective leaders understand that their behavior sets the standard for the entire organization. Leading by example involves embodying the values, work ethic, and dedication you expect from your team. If you prioritize punctuality, accountability, and innovation, your team is likely to follow suit.

Setting the tone extends beyond work habits; it's about fostering a positive and inclusive environment. Leaders who display genuine respect for diversity and demonstrate ethical decision-making create an atmosphere where employees feel valued and motivated to contribute their best.

Leading by example also means embracing transparency. Sharing successes and challenges with the team fosters a culture of openness. This transparency builds trust and encourages employees to be forthcoming with ideas, concerns, and suggestions.

Fostering a Culture of Accountability and Empowerment
Profitable businesses are built on a foundation of accountability. Leaders who cultivate a culture of accountability ensure that team members take ownership of

their responsibilities and outcomes. This involves clearly defining expectations, setting measurable goals, and providing regular feedback.

Empowerment goes hand-in-hand with accountability. Effective leaders delegate authority and grant team members the autonomy to make decisions within their roles. This not only relieves leaders of micro-management but also enables employees to innovate and contribute creatively.

One of the most powerful ways to foster accountability and empowerment is by promoting a learning culture. Leaders who encourage ongoing professional development show that growth is a continuous journey, not a destination. This culture of learning not only enhances individual skills but also leads to the collective advancement of the team.

Effective leadership is the linchpin that transforms a business into a profitable enterprise. Leaders who possess a clear vision, adaptability, empathy, and the ability to lead by example create an environment where success thrives. By setting the right tone, cultivating accountability, and empowering their teams, these leaders create a culture that not only drives profitability but also nurtures the growth and development of each individual.

Remember, as you develop your leadership skills, you're not just building a profitable business – you're shaping a legacy of achievement and impact that will resonate far beyond the bottom line. So, embrace these traits and practices, and let your leadership be the Midas touch that turns your business into a goldmine of success.

Building and Leading High-Performing Teams

In the ever-evolving landscape of business, one truth remains unwavering: the strength of your team is directly proportional to the success of your enterprise. While individual brilliance is undeniably valuable, the synergy of a high-performing team is what propels businesses toward unparalleled profitability. In this sub-chapter, we delve into the art of team construction and leadership, uncovering strategies to recruit, nurture, and empower teams that are not only functional but exceptional.

Strategies for Team Recruitment and Composition

Building a high-performing team starts with a meticulous approach to recruitment and composition. The intricate puzzle of personalities, skills, and strengths requires careful curation to achieve optimal results. When crafting your team, consider these strategies:

1. Diversity with Purpose: A successful team is a mosaic of diverse talents and perspectives. Seek individuals with varied backgrounds, skills, and experiences that complement one another. Diverse teams bring a richness of ideas, problem-solving approaches, and creativity that can set your business apart.

2. Skills Alignment: While diversity is crucial, alignment of skills with roles is equally paramount. Ensure that team members' skill sets resonate with the tasks they'll be responsible for. A balance of technical expertise and soft skills like communication and adaptability can drive both efficiency and collaboration.

3. Cultural Fit: Cultural alignment is the glue that holds a team together. Beyond skills, assess whether potential team members share your company's values and mission. A cohesive team culture fosters smoother communication, reduced conflicts, and enhanced motivation.

Creating a Collaborative and Innovative Environment
A high-performing team doesn't operate in isolation; it thrives within a collaborative and innovative ecosystem. As a leader, your role is to cultivate an environment that encourages open communication, experimentation, and creative thinking. Consider these steps:

1. Open Channels of Communication: Encourage regular and transparent communication among team members. Foster an atmosphere where ideas flow freely and feedback is welcomed. Team members should feel comfortable sharing their insights without fear of judgment.

2. Freedom to Innovate: Empower your team to explore unconventional solutions and take calculated risks. Embrace a culture where failure is viewed as a stepping stone to growth and innovation. Recognize and reward innovative ideas to reinforce this behavior.

3. Cross-Functional Collaboration: Break down silos by promoting collaboration across departments and disciplines. Cross-functional teams expose members to diverse perspectives and skill sets, fostering a holistic approach to problem-solving.

Conflict Resolution and Team Motivation Techniques
Where there are people, there will be differences of opinion and occasional conflicts. The art of high-performing team leadership lies in addressing conflicts constructively and keeping motivation levels high. Consider these strategies:

1. Constructive Conflict Resolution: Conflict is an opportunity for growth when managed effectively. Encourage open dialogues, active listening, and empathy when conflicts arise. Aim for win-win resolutions that strengthen relationships rather than fostering resentments.

2. Recognition and Appreciation: Regularly acknowledge the efforts and accomplishments of your team members. Public recognition and tangible rewards not only boost morale but also cultivate a sense of ownership and pride in their work.

3. Goal Alignment: Ensure that every team member understands the overarching goals of the project and how their contributions fit into the larger picture. This clarity of purpose motivates individuals to work collaboratively and go the extra mile.

The art of building and leading high-performing teams transcends simple management—it's an intricate dance of understanding, empowerment, and inspiration. By thoughtfully assembling diverse talents, fostering a collaborative environment, and navigating conflicts with finesse, you'll unlock the full potential of your team, propelling your business toward unprecedented profitability and success.

Remember, the synergy of a team is not solely a product of individual brilliance; it's the harmonious orchestration of these distinct talents that creates a symphony of success. Harness the Midas Touch of effective leadership, and watch your teams turn challenges into opportunities, and opportunities into profit.

Developing Succession Plans for Business Continuity

In the ever-evolving landscape of business, effective leadership is paramount to success. But true success is not merely defined by the accomplishments of a current leader; it's measured by the ability of an organization to seamlessly transition from one capable leader to another. This is where succession planning comes into play—a strategic process that ensures business continuity and sustainability by identifying, grooming, and preparing the next generation of leaders.

Importance of Grooming Future Leaders

Grooming future leaders is not a luxury; it's a necessity. Businesses that fail to cultivate leadership talent risk facing a leadership vacuum when key figures step down or move on. Succession planning is like planting seeds that will grow into strong, capable trees, ensuring that when the time comes, the organization can carry on its mission and maintain its profitability without skipping a beat.

Forward-thinking businesses recognize that the skills, insights, and experience that make current leaders effective should be passed on. By investing in grooming future leaders, companies not only safeguard their continuity but also foster a culture of growth and development, motivating employees to excel and contribute with a sense of purpose.

Identifying and Nurturing Leadership Potential

Identifying potential leaders is a skill that requires careful observation and an eye for potential. Look beyond the obvious traits—while charisma and assertiveness have their merits, qualities like empathy, adaptability, and the ability to inspire are equally crucial. Potential leaders are those who exhibit a keen understanding of the business, a commitment to its values, and the drive to innovate and push boundaries.

Nurturing leadership potential involves mentorship, training, and tailored developmental opportunities. Assigning aspiring leaders to cross-functional teams, offering stretch assignments, and encouraging participation in leadership programs all contribute to their growth. An effective approach is to create a roadmap that outlines the skills and experiences needed for leadership roles, guiding individuals through a holistic development journey.

Ensuring a Smooth Transition During Leadership Changes

Leadership transitions can be turbulent if not handled meticulously. Succession planning aims to smoothen this process, ensuring that the transfer of power is not only seamless but also inspiring. A well-prepared successor steps into their role with confidence, armed with a deep understanding of the organization's goals, strategies, and culture.

Transparent communication is a linchpin during leadership changes. Both incoming and outgoing leaders need to communicate openly about their visions, strategies, and expectations. This continuity of vision reassures employees and stakeholders that the organization's trajectory remains steady.

Additionally, cross-training and shadowing experiences can provide successors with hands-on exposure to the responsibilities of their future roles. These experiences bridge the gap between theory and practice, allowing them to apply their skills and insights to real-world scenarios before officially assuming their roles.

Succession planning also extends beyond the initial transition. Regular check-ins, mentorship, and ongoing support from outgoing leaders can aid in the ongoing development of new leaders. This creates a symbiotic relationship where the wisdom of seasoned leaders combines with the fresh perspectives of emerging ones, creating a potent recipe for innovation and success.

Developing succession plans for business continuity is not a luxury—it's a strategic imperative. Businesses that invest in grooming future leaders, identifying and nurturing leadership potential, and ensuring smooth transitions safeguard their profitability and long-term growth. Effective leadership transcends the individual; it's about ensuring that the organization thrives today, tomorrow, and for years to come. As you embark on this journey of cultivating leaders, remember that your commitment to succession planning shapes not only your organization's future but the future of the business landscape itself.

Chapter 11: Global Expansion and International Profitability

Assessing Readiness for International Expansion

In today's interconnected world, the allure of global expansion is undeniable. The prospect of tapping into new markets, reaching diverse audiences, and boosting profitability can be truly enticing. However, before taking the leap into international waters, businesses must meticulously evaluate their preparedness for such a strategic move. This sub-chapter delves into the critical aspects of assessing your organization's readiness for international expansion, ensuring that your journey to global profitability is well-calculated and successful.

Analyzing Market Potential and Cultural Factors

Before venturing into new markets, a thorough analysis of market potential is paramount. As the business adage goes, "If you fail to plan, you plan to fail." Evaluating the potential demand for your products or services in a foreign market requires a comprehensive understanding of the target audience's preferences, needs, and purchasing power.

Market research becomes your compass in this endeavor. Utilize both qualitative and quantitative research methods to decipher local consumer behavior, market trends, and competitive landscape. A nuanced understanding of cultural factors, such as language, customs, and cultural sensitivities, is equally vital. Crafting strategies that resonate with the local culture and customs can substantially enhance your chances of success.

Furthermore, engaging with local experts and consultants can provide invaluable insights into the intricacies of the market. By investing time and resources into understanding the nuances of your target market, you set the stage for an informed and effective global expansion.

Evaluating Legal and Regulatory Challenges
The regulatory landscape can vary significantly from one country to another, and understanding the legal complexities is essential to avoid potential pitfalls. It's prudent to conduct a thorough legal analysis to ensure compliance with local laws and regulations, intellectual property protection, and tax requirements. Engage legal professionals with expertise in international business to navigate through the legal intricacies of your chosen market.

Trade agreements, tariffs, and import/export regulations can impact your profitability and operational efficiency. Being well-versed in these aspects helps you make informed decisions about pricing, logistics, and overall strategy. Moreover, understanding employment laws and labor regulations is crucial when establishing a local workforce, ensuring ethical and legal employment practices.

Strategic Planning for Global Growth

Global expansion is not just about dipping your toes in international waters; it's a strategic endeavor that requires meticulous planning. The blueprint for your global growth should encompass various dimensions, including marketing, operations, supply chain, and finance.

Developing a clear and executable international business plan is fundamental. Set specific objectives and delineate actionable steps to achieve them. A robust financial analysis should underpin your strategy, outlining the investments required, projected revenues, and potential risks. Adequate financial forecasting enables you to allocate resources effectively, plan for contingencies, and maintain profitability despite uncertainties.

Collaboration across teams is pivotal during this phase. Marketing teams should adapt strategies to align with local preferences, while supply chain and operations teams must address logistical challenges. Effective communication and a streamlined decision-making process can smoothen the complexities of international expansion.

International expansion presents a spectrum of opportunities and challenges. While the allure of global profitability is compelling, a systematic and thorough approach is paramount. Analyzing market potential, understanding cultural dynamics, navigating legal intricacies, and strategic planning are the cornerstones of a successful global expansion. By building a foundation on these principles, businesses can leverage the vast potential of global markets while safeguarding profitability and sustainability. Remember, the key to international success is not only in the destination but also in the journey of preparation and adaptability.

Navigating International Business Operations

In today's interconnected world, expanding a business beyond borders presents both lucrative opportunities and complex challenges. Navigating international business operations requires a strategic approach that factors in cultural nuances, logistical considerations, and adaptability. In this sub-chapter, we will delve into the key components of effectively navigating international business operations to ensure successful global expansion.

Establishing Effective Distribution and Logistics

One of the fundamental pillars of international business success lies in establishing a robust distribution and logistics network. The intricacies of cross-border supply chains demand meticulous planning and execution. Efficiently delivering products or services to your target markets requires addressing several critical aspects:

- **Localization of Supply Chain**: Tailoring your supply chain to accommodate local preferences, regulations, and infrastructure is paramount. Collaborating with local partners who possess a deep understanding of the market can streamline the process.

- **Risk Management**: International logistics can be subject to disruptions such as customs delays, geopolitical tensions, and natural disasters. Developing contingency plans and diversifying suppliers and transportation modes can mitigate these risks.

- **Technology Integration**: Incorporating advanced tracking technologies and data analytics ensures transparency and traceability throughout the supply chain, aiding in optimizing routes and minimizing lead times.

Overcoming Language and Communication Barriers
Clear communication serves as the cornerstone of successful international business operations. Language barriers can hinder effective collaboration and customer engagement. Here are key strategies to overcome these challenges:

- **Localization of Communication**: Tailoring your marketing materials, website, and customer communications to the local language and culture can significantly enhance your market penetration. This conveys respect for the local audience and builds rapport.

- **Cultural Sensitivity**: Understanding cultural nuances in communication is crucial. What may be considered polite in one culture could be perceived differently in another. Investing in cross-cultural training for your team can foster better communication.

- **Multilingual Support**: Providing multilingual customer support can enhance customer satisfaction and loyalty.

Utilizing translation services, chatbots, and multilingual staff can bridge communication gaps effectively.

Adapting Products and Services for Diverse Markets
A vital aspect of international success lies in adapting your offerings to resonate with diverse markets. What appeals to one culture might not resonate with another. Here's how to tailor your products and services effectively:

- **Market Research**: Conduct thorough market research to identify local preferences, needs, and trends. This knowledge can guide product modifications or the introduction of new offerings.

- **Localization vs. Standardization**: Striking a balance between localization and standardization is essential. While adapting products to suit local tastes is crucial, maintaining a consistent brand identity can foster global recognition.

- **Regulatory Compliance**: Be aware of local regulations and compliance requirements that may affect your product or service. Ensure that your offerings meet legal standards without compromising quality.

Navigating international business operations demands a comprehensive approach that encompasses distribution, communication, and adaptation. Successful global expansion hinges on understanding the intricacies of each target market and strategically aligning your business operations with their unique demands. By establishing effective distribution networks, overcoming language barriers, and adapting products and services intelligently, you can position your business for profitability on the global stage. Remember, cultural sensitivity, flexibility, and a commitment to continuous learning are your tools for triumph in the realm of international business.

Managing Cross-Border Financials and Risk

In today's interconnected global economy, expanding your business internationally can unlock a world of opportunities, but it also presents a host of financial complexities and risks. Navigating the challenges of managing cross-border financials is a crucial aspect of international business success. In this sub-chapter, we will delve deep into the intricacies of currency fluctuations, international taxation, and the strategies to expand profit margins in global markets.

Currency Fluctuations and Risk Mitigation Strategies

Currency fluctuations, often driven by macroeconomic factors, geopolitical events, and market sentiment, can significantly impact your business's profitability when operating across borders. As exchange rates fluctuate, the value of your earnings in your home currency can vary, directly influencing your bottom line. To manage these risks, it's essential to implement effective currency risk mitigation strategies.

One approach is hedging, which involves using financial instruments like forward contracts or options to lock in exchange rates for future transactions. This shields your business from sudden shifts in currency values. Additionally, diversifying your operations across multiple markets can help offset currency-related losses in one region with gains in another.

International Taxation and Compliance Considerations
Entering international markets introduces complex tax implications that can't be ignored. Each jurisdiction has its own tax laws, treaties, and regulations governing corporate taxation, withholding taxes, and more. To ensure compliance and minimize tax liabilities, it's imperative to enlist the expertise of international tax professionals who can navigate these intricacies.

Transfer pricing is another critical aspect of international taxation. This involves determining the prices for transactions between related entities in different countries. Staying in line with transfer pricing regulations is vital to avoid disputes with tax authorities and maintain a transparent and compliant global operation.

Expanding Profit Margins in Global Markets
Expanding profit margins while operating in global markets requires a multifaceted approach that combines strategic planning, market adaptation, and operational efficiency. Here are some strategies to consider:

1. Localization: Customize your products or services to cater to the specific preferences and needs of each market. Adapting your offerings can enhance customer satisfaction and drive higher profit margins.

2. Pricing Strategies: Conduct thorough market research to determine the pricing dynamics in each target market. Consider factors like local purchasing power, competition, and perceived value to set optimal prices that maximize profitability.

3. Supply Chain Optimization: Streamline your supply chain to reduce costs and increase efficiency. This might involve sourcing materials locally to avoid import duties or collaborating with local distributors to cut down on transportation costs.

4. Leverage Economies of Scale: As your international presence grows, explore opportunities to centralize certain operations or functions. This can lead to cost savings through economies of scale.

5. Strategic Partnerships: Collaborate with local partners to navigate market nuances effectively. These partnerships can provide insights into local customer behavior, distribution networks, and regulatory requirements.

6. Risk Management: Implement robust risk management strategies to address potential disruptions, whether they arise from political instability, economic downturns, or other unforeseen events.

Global expansion holds immense potential for increased profitability, but it also comes with intricate financial challenges and risks. By carefully navigating currency fluctuations, adhering to international tax regulations, and adopting effective profit-enhancing strategies, your business can thrive in the global marketplace. As you embark on this journey, remember that a well-informed approach and a thorough understanding of global financial dynamics are your keys to international success.

Chapter 12: Sustainable Practices for Long-Term Profitability

Embracing Corporate Social Responsibility (CSR)

In the contemporary business landscape, where the pursuit of profit often coincides with social and environmental concerns, the concept of Corporate Social Responsibility (CSR) has gained paramount significance. The integration of ethical and sustainable practices into business strategies has proven to be more than just a moral obligation—it is a strategic imperative that brings about a positive impact on brand reputation and profitability. In this sub chapter, we will delve into the profound importance of CSR, explore the ways to seamlessly integrate it into business operations, and uncover the symbiotic relationship between CSR, brand equity, and financial success.

Importance of Ethical and Sustainable Practices

Corporate Social Responsibility, often referred to as the "triple bottom line" approach, emphasizes three key dimensions: people, planet, and profit. This holistic perspective recognizes that businesses have an inherent responsibility not only to generate economic value but also to contribute positively to society and safeguard the environment. Ethical and sustainable practices are not merely altruistic gestures; they play a pivotal role in building trust, enhancing stakeholder loyalty, and securing long-term profitability.

Consumers today are more conscious than ever before about the ethical and environmental implications of their purchasing decisions. They are drawn to businesses that align with their values and contribute positively to the world. By practicing CSR, businesses create a virtuous cycle: their efforts to make a difference resonate with consumers, leading to increased brand loyalty, higher sales, and ultimately, greater profitability. Furthermore, responsible practices can lead to operational efficiencies, cost savings, and improved risk management, all of which directly contribute to the bottom line.

Integrating CSR into Business Strategies
The integration of CSR into business strategies is not a superficial exercise; it requires a strategic mindset that considers social and environmental considerations as intrinsic components of decision-making. To successfully implement CSR, businesses must conduct a thorough assessment of their operations, identifying areas where positive change can be effected. This might involve reducing carbon emissions, optimizing resource utilization, promoting diversity and inclusion, or engaging in community development initiatives.

Importantly, CSR initiatives should align with the core values and mission of the business. When CSR efforts are authentic and aligned with the company's purpose, they resonate more strongly with stakeholders and have a more profound impact on brand perception. For instance, a sportswear brand that prioritizes sustainability in its supply chain communicates its commitment to the environment not only through words but also through actions.

Positive Impact on Brand Reputation and Profit
The interplay between CSR, brand reputation, and profit is a dynamic relationship that highlights the interconnectedness of these elements. Engaging in socially responsible practices enhances a business's brand reputation by showcasing its commitment to addressing societal challenges. Consumers view such businesses as responsible, trustworthy, and caring, which strengthens their emotional connection with the brand. This emotional resonance translates into greater customer loyalty, repeat business, and positive word-of-mouth referrals.

Moreover, the positive image established through CSR initiatives serves as a competitive differentiator. In a saturated market, where products and services can be easily commoditized, a strong brand built on ethical principles stands out. Customers are willing to pay a premium for products and services associated with companies that make a meaningful impact beyond profit generation. This willingness to pay more translates into improved profit margins and financial performance.

Embracing Corporate Social Responsibility is not just a moral obligation; it is a strategic pathway to long-term profitability. Ethical and sustainable practices resonate with consumers, strengthen brand reputation, and foster enduring loyalty. Integrating CSR into business strategies aligns values with actions, creating a virtuous cycle of positive impact and financial success. As businesses navigate the evolving marketplace, those that authentically embrace CSR are poised to not only thrive financially but also leave a lasting legacy of positive change.

Eco-Friendly Innovation for Profit and Planet

In an era defined by rapidly evolving markets and growing environmental concerns, the convergence of profitability and sustainability has emerged as a cornerstone of successful business strategies. The imperative to embrace eco-friendly practices isn't merely an ethical obligation but a strategic necessity. Companies that prioritize sustainability are not only contributing to a healthier planet but also positioning themselves for long-term profitability and resilience.

Leveraging Green Technologies and Practices

The marriage of profit and planet starts with the adoption of green technologies and practices. Organizations that embrace renewable energy sources, energy-efficient processes, and eco-friendly materials experience a dual benefit. By integrating solar panels, wind turbines, and energy-efficient lighting, companies can drastically reduce energy costs while demonstrating their commitment to a sustainable future. The initial investment in these technologies is often recouped through substantial savings in operational expenses over time.

Furthermore, adopting sustainable supply chain practices can minimize the environmental impact of production and distribution. Implementing strategies such as sourcing materials from ethical suppliers, reducing waste through recycling and upcycling, and optimizing transportation routes not only mitigate environmental harm but also streamline operations, leading to cost savings and enhanced customer perception.

Reducing Environmental Footprint and Costs
Sustainability isn't solely about embracing new technologies—it's also about rethinking and optimizing existing processes. Businesses that commit to reducing their environmental footprint often find opportunities for cost reduction that lead to increased profitability.

Minimizing waste through lean manufacturing principles not only conserves resources but also reduces expenses associated with waste disposal. This strategy enhances operational efficiency and enables companies to redirect funds toward growth-oriented endeavors.

Additionally, remote work and digital communication technologies can significantly diminish the need for physical office space and extensive travel. This reduction in overhead expenses, combined with the environmental benefits of reduced commuting and emissions, positions organizations for a dual advantage: cost savings and a smaller carbon footprint.

Marketing Sustainability Efforts for Profit Growth

Effective marketing of sustainability initiatives can yield substantial gains, both financially and in terms of brand loyalty. Today's consumers are increasingly environmentally conscious and are more likely to support brands that align with their values. Transparent communication of a company's commitment to eco-friendly practices resonates positively with customers, creating a deeper emotional connection and engendering brand loyalty.

Investing in sustainability also opens doors to new markets. As global awareness of environmental issues grows, many consumers actively seek out businesses that prioritize sustainable practices. Companies that position themselves as leaders in eco-friendly innovation can capture a share of this expanding market, leading to increased revenues and enhanced profit margins.

The marketing value of sustainability extends beyond consumers to potential investors. Many investors consider a company's environmental and social performance as a factor in their decisions. Demonstrating a robust commitment to sustainability can attract ethical and impact investors who align their financial choices with their values.

Eco-friendly innovation isn't merely a trend; it's a fundamental shift in how businesses operate. The convergence of profitability and sustainability isn't a trade-off, but a symbiotic relationship. As your business reduces its environmental impact, it's simultaneously enhancing operational efficiency and lowering costs. Communicating these efforts to stakeholders enhances your brand's reputation and drives customer loyalty. The road to long-term profitability lies in embracing sustainability as a core business strategy—a strategy that leads to a better planet and a healthier bottom line.

Social Entrepreneurship and Profitable Impact

In today's rapidly changing business landscape, the concept of profit has evolved beyond financial gains. As entrepreneurs and business leaders, we now recognize the significance of balancing profit with a broader impact on society and the environment. This shift has given rise to a remarkable phenomenon known as social entrepreneurship – a potent fusion of business acumen and societal betterment. In this sub-chapter, we will delve deep into the world of social entrepreneurship, exploring how it harmoniously intertwines profitability with positive impact, backed by case studies of successful enterprises and strategies for effective measurement and expansion.

Balancing Profit with Social and Environmental Impact
Social entrepreneurship stands at the crossroads of business innovation and social change. It embodies a dual purpose: creating sustainable profits while addressing pressing societal and environmental challenges. This dynamic balance is what propels social enterprises into the heart of meaningful transformation. Unlike traditional businesses, where profit is often the sole measure of success, social enterprises adopt a broader perspective that intertwines financial gain with the well-being of people and the planet.

Imagine a world where a business's success is not solely measured by its financial bottom line but by its positive contributions to society. This is precisely what social entrepreneurs aspire to achieve. By innovating products and services that provide solutions to real-world problems – from poverty and access to clean water to education and healthcare – they redefine profit to encompass the invaluable currency of positive change.

Case Studies of Successful Social Enterprises
The impact of social entrepreneurship is exemplified by a host of successful enterprises that have seamlessly integrated profit with purpose. Take, for instance, TOMS Shoes, a company that pioneered the "One for One" model. For every pair of shoes sold, TOMS donates a pair to a child in need. This ingenious business model not only drove sales but also provided footwear to countless underprivileged children worldwide, demonstrating that profitability and altruism can go hand in hand.

Another inspiring example is Grameen Bank, founded by Nobel laureate Muhammad Yunus. This microfinance institution provides loans to the impoverished, enabling them to start small businesses and break the cycle of poverty. By addressing social inequalities through financial empowerment, Grameen Bank showcases how profit-driven endeavors can profoundly impact communities.

Strategies for Measuring and Scaling Impact
While the intersection of profit and social impact is profound, measuring and scaling this impact presents its own set of challenges. However, social entrepreneurs have devised innovative strategies to gauge and amplify their influence. The use of metrics like the Social Return on Investment (SROI) allows businesses to quantify their contributions to society in monetary terms, enabling them to demonstrate a return not only in financial gains but also in social well-being.

Moreover, scaling impact involves replicating successful models across regions and industries. An exemplary approach is embraced by Ashoka, a global organization that identifies and supports leading social entrepreneurs. Ashoka's Fellows represent a network of change-makers who have crafted scalable solutions to various challenges, ranging from education to healthcare. By harnessing the power of collaboration and knowledge-sharing, these entrepreneurs amplify their impact far beyond their immediate reach.

The era of social entrepreneurship marks a transformative shift in how we perceive profit and its potential for meaningful change. By striking a harmonious balance between profitability and positive societal and environmental impact, social entrepreneurs inspire a new breed of businesses that measure success through multifaceted lenses. Through the lens of case studies, we witness how the innovative spirit of entrepreneurs can drive solutions to some of the world's most pressing problems. As we navigate this landscape, the strategies for measuring and scaling impact empower us to cultivate lasting change, one business venture at a time. Remember, the essence of social entrepreneurship lies not just in the products or services offered, but in the lives touched, the communities uplifted, and the legacy of profit intertwined with purpose.

Chapter 13: Competitive Differentiation and Branding

Crafting a Distinctive Brand Identity

In the ever-evolving landscape of modern business, where competition is fierce and attention spans are fleeting, crafting a distinctive brand identity is not just a marketing strategy—it's a survival imperative. A powerful brand identity serves as the cornerstone upon which businesses build lasting relationships with their audience, resonate with their values, and leave an indelible mark on their collective consciousness. In this sub-chapter, we delve into the art and science of creating a brand identity that not only captivates but also drives profitability.

Defining Brand Values and Mission

At the heart of a strong brand identity lies a clear and resolute sense of purpose. Defining brand values and mission goes beyond the mere delineation of abstract concepts; it's about articulating the core beliefs that your business stands for. These values aren't just statements—they are guiding principles that permeate every facet of your operations. Consider what your business truly believes in. Is it innovation, reliability, sustainability, or perhaps customer empowerment? Unearthing and expressing these values serves as a magnetic force that attracts like-minded customers who share your vision.

Furthermore, crafting a compelling mission statement is akin to plotting the course of your brand's journey. It's a concise, yet potent, declaration of your purpose and the impact you aspire to make. Your mission statement isn't just for the company's wall; it's a rally cry that resonates with your employees and customers alike. The alchemy of brand values and mission creates a foundation upon which customer loyalty, employee dedication, and profit potential flourish.

Creating a Memorable Brand Visual Identity
In a world dominated by visual stimuli, a memorable brand visual identity is the gateway to recognition and recall. Your visual identity isn't merely a logo; it's a cohesive ensemble of design elements that work harmoniously to convey your brand's personality, essence, and promise. From color palettes to typography, every detail matters. Your brand's colors can evoke emotions, and your chosen typeface can communicate seriousness or playfulness.

Consider the golden arches of a certain fast-food chain or the swoosh of a renowned sportswear company. These iconic symbols transcend language and culture—they speak a universal visual language. A successful visual identity creates an instant association with your brand, even before a single word is read or spoken.

Aligning Brand with Customer Perception
The true power of a brand identity emerges when it aligns seamlessly with the perception your customers hold. This alignment fosters trust, as customers recognize a

congruence between your brand's promises and the experiences they encounter. However, brand perception isn't merely a one-way street—it's an ongoing dialogue. To shape customer perception, you must consistently deliver on your brand promises, exceed expectations, and adapt to changing customer needs.

Social media, reviews, and word-of-mouth play pivotal roles in shaping brand perception. A single negative experience can ripple across digital platforms, tarnishing the image you've worked diligently to build. Conversely, a string of positive interactions can solidify your brand's reputation as one that delivers value consistently.

In the realm of brand identity, alignment extends beyond visuals and transcends into emotions. What does your brand make customers feel? Is it trust, excitement, comfort, or a combination? Delving into these emotions and shaping them purposefully enhances your brand's impact.

Crafting a distinctive brand identity requires a deep understanding of your business's core values, an eye for design that encapsulates your essence, and an unwavering commitment to aligning perception with reality. In an era where choices are abundant and loyalty is hard-won, a brand identity that strikes a chord with authenticity can be the Midas touch that turns fleeting attention into devoted, long-lasting patronage. Remember, your brand identity is not just a logo—it's the story of your business, the emotions it evokes, and the legacy it leaves behind.

As you embark on this journey of branding, remember that a strong brand identity isn't a static artifact; it's a living entity that evolves alongside your business and resonates with the aspirations of your target audience. By forging an authentic and memorable brand identity, you're not just differentiating yourself—you're creating an enduring relationship with your customers that transcends transactional exchanges and transcends into the realm of meaningful, profitable engagement.

Effective Brand Positioning for Profitable Impact

In the fast-paced and competitive landscape of business, where numerous players vie for consumer attention, the significance of effective brand positioning cannot be overstated. Brand positioning is the art of defining a unique space in the minds of consumers, setting your business apart from the competition and creating a powerful emotional connection that resonates with your target audience. In this sub-chapter, we delve deep into the strategies and tactics that allow businesses to leverage brand positioning for a lasting and profitable impact.

Identifying Your Unique Value Proposition (UVP)

At the heart of successful brand positioning lies a crystal-clear understanding of your Unique Value Proposition (UVP). Your UVP encapsulates what makes your business distinct, valuable, and worthy of consumer consideration. It answers the fundamental question: "Why should customers choose you over your competitors?"

To identify your UVP, begin by conducting a comprehensive analysis of your offerings, strengths, and market positioning. What problems does your product or service solve? What benefits do you offer that no one else does? Your UVP should be specific, succinct, and aligned with the needs and desires of your target audience. It serves as your brand's North Star, guiding all aspects of your business, from product development to marketing campaigns.

Targeting the Right Market Segment
Even the most innovative products or services won't generate substantial profits if they aren't reaching the right audience. This is where precise market segmentation comes into play. Rather than trying to appeal to a broad audience, identify specific segments that are most likely to resonate with your brand's value proposition.

Segmentation can be based on demographics (age, gender, income), psychographics (values, lifestyle), behavior (buying patterns), or even geographic location. By understanding the unique preferences and pain points of each segment, you can tailor your messaging and offerings to resonate deeply. This targeted approach not only enhances the relevance of your brand but also increases the likelihood of profitable conversions.

Creating an Emotional Connection through Branding

In a world inundated with choices, consumers don't just buy products or services; they buy experiences and emotions. Effective branding goes beyond logos and colors; it's about cultivating a genuine emotional connection between your brand and your customers. A powerful brand elicits emotions that forge loyalty, advocacy, and long-term relationships.

To create such a connection, your branding must align with your UVP and resonate with the emotions of your target audience. Whether it's a sense of belonging, security, or aspiration, your brand should evoke emotions that drive consumers to choose you over alternatives. This emotional resonance forms the cornerstone of brand loyalty, leading to repeat business and positive word-of-mouth marketing.

As you craft your brand's emotional narrative, consider storytelling as a potent tool. Share the journey, values, and principles that define your business. Paint a vivid picture of the impact you aspire to make in your customers' lives. Remember, people don't just buy products; they buy into stories that mirror their own aspirations and values.

Effective brand positioning is the linchpin of business success. It's not merely about standing out; it's about standing out for the right reasons and leaving an indelible mark in the hearts and minds of consumers. By identifying your UVP, targeting the right market segments, and crafting a compelling emotional connection, you can position your brand for profitability and long-term growth.

Remember, brand positioning isn't a one-time endeavor; it's an ongoing process that requires adaptation, innovation, and a relentless commitment to delivering value. Through this strategic approach to branding, you can unlock the true potential of your business and leave an enduring mark on the competitive landscape.

Brand Reputation Management for Long-Term Success

In the fast-paced and interconnected world of business, building a solid brand reputation isn't just a buzzword – it's a strategic imperative. Your brand's reputation serves as the bedrock of your long-term success, shaping how customers perceive your business, influencing their purchasing decisions, and ultimately impacting your bottom line. In this sub-chapter, we delve deep into the art and science of brand reputation management, exploring how to cultivate and preserve brand trust, navigate PR crises, and strategically leverage positive associations for sustainable profitability.

Building and Maintaining Brand Trust

Trust is the currency of the modern business landscape. Customers no longer base their purchasing decisions solely on product features; they also consider the integrity and authenticity of the brands behind those products. Building brand trust involves consistent and transparent communication, aligning your actions with your brand promise, and demonstrating genuine concern for your customers' needs.

Transparency is paramount. From product sourcing to operational practices, sharing insights into your business processes not only fosters trust but also showcases your commitment to ethical business conduct. A comprehensive and accessible privacy policy and terms of service demonstrate respect for your customers' data and rights, further solidifying your reputation as a trustworthy brand.

Handling PR Crises and Negative Feedback
In the era of social media and instant communication, even the most well-established brands can find themselves in the eye of a PR storm. The key to managing a crisis is preparation and timely response. Anticipating potential issues and having a crisis management plan in place helps you react swiftly and effectively.

When facing negative feedback or a PR crisis, a proactive response is essential. Acknowledge the concern openly, express empathy, and offer a solution. This not only mitigates damage but also showcases your commitment to customer satisfaction. Remember, a well-handled crisis can actually enhance your reputation if it demonstrates your dedication to addressing challenges head-on.

Leveraging Positive Brand Associations for Profit

Your brand associations – the emotions, perceptions, and memories tied to your brand – are powerful tools for profitability. Positive associations can lead to increased customer loyalty, higher brand recall, and even premium pricing. Leveraging these associations requires a comprehensive branding strategy that focuses on consistency and alignment.

To harness positive brand associations, consider brand partnerships that resonate with your values and appeal to your target audience. Collaborative efforts can amplify your message and introduce your brand to new audiences, contributing to both brand awareness and profitability.

Furthermore, capitalize on storytelling to humanize your brand. Share success stories, customer testimonials, and anecdotes that reflect your brand's impact on people's lives. Authenticity in storytelling builds emotional connections, reinforcing positive associations that drive customer loyalty.

In today's hyper-competitive business landscape, brand reputation management is a cornerstone of sustained success. Building trust, effectively navigating crises, and strategically leveraging positive associations are not only critical for immediate profitability but also for long-term growth. As you embark on the journey of cultivating a powerful brand reputation, remember that consistency, transparency, and customer-centricity are the pillars that uphold your brand's value and contribute to your Midas Touch in the world of business.

Chapter 14: The Power of Networking and Partnerships

Developing Profitable Business Relationships

In the intricate tapestry of the modern business landscape, the power of networking and partnerships shines brightly as a cornerstone of success. As entrepreneurs and business leaders, we tread a path that is as much about building bridges as it is about creating products and services. The ability to forge strong and strategic relationships has evolved from being a mere advantage to becoming an indispensable component of achieving sustainable growth. In this subchapter, we delve into the profound significance of networking for growth, the art of cultivating authentic connections with industry peers, and the transformational potential of leveraging partnerships for mutual benefit.

Importance of Networking for Growth

Networking is akin to a well-orchestrated symphony where each note resonates, contributing to the harmonious progress of your business. The importance of networking for growth cannot be overstated. In a world increasingly defined by connectivity, the relationships you nurture have the potential to open doors, unlock opportunities, and provide you with access to insights that can propel your business forward.

Networking is more than simply exchanging business cards at conferences or industry events. It's about fostering genuine connections that transcend transactional exchanges. By interacting with peers, industry leaders, and potential collaborators, you expose yourself to diverse perspectives, novel ideas, and invaluable knowledge. These interactions can spark innovation, challenge your assumptions, and lead to partnerships that have the potential to redefine your business trajectory.

Building Genuine Connections with Industry Peers
In the age of digital communication, the art of building genuine connections may seem challenged. However, the truth remains that relationships built on authenticity, trust, and mutual respect have the power to transcend screens and resonate deeply. When interacting with industry peers, focus on meaningful engagement rather than a mere exchange of pleasantries.

Listen attentively to others' stories, challenges, and successes. Empathy and understanding go a long way in fostering strong connections. Instead of approaching interactions with a transactional mindset, seek to add value to the lives of those you meet. Sharing insights, offering assistance, or connecting people with resources that can benefit them fosters goodwill and lays the foundation for lasting relationships.

Leveraging Partnerships for Mutual Benefit
Partnerships stand as a testament to the fact that collaboration often yields results greater than the sum of individual efforts. In the dynamic business environment,

where agility and innovation are prized, partnerships offer a compelling avenue for growth. A well-forged partnership can provide complementary strengths, shared resources, and extended market reach.

To leverage partnerships for mutual benefit, a strategic approach is paramount. Before entering into a partnership, consider your compatibility in terms of values, goals, and vision. Clearly define the objectives of the partnership and how each party stands to gain. Communication is key; transparency and open dialogue build trust and help navigate potential challenges.

Moreover, partnerships aren't confined to traditional B2B collaborations. Consider exploring partnerships with suppliers, customers, or even organizations outside your industry that share a common target audience. These partnerships can facilitate cross-promotion, enhance customer experiences, and diversify revenue streams.

The art of networking and forging partnerships is a dynamic force that propels businesses beyond boundaries. Embrace networking as a tool for growth, not just for your business, but for your personal growth as well. Seek authentic connections with industry peers that transcend the transactional, and be open to partnerships that can amplify your impact. The tapestry of business relationships you weave today will shape the legacy you leave behind—a legacy of growth, innovation, and meaningful impact.

Collaborative Innovation and Co-Creation

In the dynamic landscape of modern business, success is no longer solely achieved through isolated efforts. The age-old adage "two heads are better than one" has never rung truer, as the strategic deployment of collaborative innovation and co-creation emerges as a driving force behind profitable growth. In this sub chapter, we delve into the profound impact that harnessing the power of collaboration, engaging in joint ventures, and fostering strategic alliances can have on elevating your business to new heights of profitability.

Harnessing the Power of Collaboration

In today's interconnected world, the boundaries between companies, industries, and even geographies have blurred, giving rise to a culture of collaboration that transcends traditional competition. Collaborative innovation is the art of leveraging collective intelligence, resources, and expertise to generate novel solutions, accelerate product development, and enhance customer experiences. By engaging with partners who bring diverse perspectives and complementary strengths to the table, businesses can break through innovation barriers that might otherwise prove insurmountable.

Effective collaboration extends beyond internal teams, encompassing external stakeholders such as customers, suppliers, and even competitors. This approach not only fosters innovation but also bolsters trust and creates a symbiotic ecosystem where each participant stands to gain. Moreover, collaboration often leads to knowledge-sharing, reducing redundancy, and amplifying the speed of ideation and implementation. The concept of open innovation, popularized by business thought leaders, demonstrates that a collaborative mindset is the catalyst for progress and profitability in today's interconnected world.

Joint Ventures and Strategic Alliances

While collaboration nurtures incremental innovation, joint ventures (JVs) and strategic alliances open the gateway to exponential growth and profit. JVs involve the coming together of two or more companies to form a separate entity, pooling resources, risks, and rewards. This approach allows for shared investments in high-risk, high-reward projects that might be unfeasible for a single entity. Strategic alliances, on the other hand, are agreements between two or more entities to work together on a project without forming a separate legal entity. Both JVs and strategic alliances enable businesses to tap into new markets, leverage distribution channels, and access specialized capabilities.

The key to successful JVs and alliances lies in a carefully cultivated synergy. The partnering entities must align their objectives, vision, and operational methodologies to ensure seamless collaboration. Clearly defined roles, responsibilities, and expectations are crucial to prevent misunderstandings and potential conflicts down the line. In the realm of innovation, JVs and alliances act as a vehicle for pooling expertise and resources to develop groundbreaking products or services that can capture new market segments and drive significant revenue.

Innovating Through Partnerships for Profit
The pursuit of innovation is a perpetual quest for businesses seeking a competitive edge and sustainable profitability. However, innovation need not be a solitary endeavor. Partnerships have the potential to ignite creativity, fuel breakthroughs, and generate profits that would be unattainable in isolation.

When businesses collaborate, their collective knowledge becomes greater than the sum of its parts. This dynamic synergy often leads to the co-creation of solutions that neither party could have conceived individually. Co-creation involves actively involving customers, partners, and stakeholders in the innovation process, ensuring that products and services are tailor-made to meet genuine needs.

Strategic partnerships can also expedite time-to-market, reducing development cycles and positioning products for profit more swiftly. Moreover, innovation through collaboration enhances risk management. With a diversified pool of resources and expertise, the burden of unforeseen challenges is distributed, allowing businesses to navigate uncertainties with greater resilience.

The power of collaboration, joint ventures, and strategic alliances is an undeniable force that can propel businesses toward unprecedented profitability. These approaches foster an environment where innovation thrives, risks are mitigated, and resources are maximized. The dynamic interplay of diverse perspectives and collective expertise holds the potential to shape industries, disrupt markets, and redefine the very essence of business success.

In the realm of collaborative innovation and co-creation, there is no shortage of success stories. From tech giants forging strategic partnerships to deliver cutting-edge solutions to startups forming joint ventures to penetrate new markets, the power of working together is evident across industries. As you embark on this transformative journey, remember that the essence of profitable collaboration lies not only in the agreements and ventures but in the mindset that fuels them—a mindset that embraces the idea that by working together, businesses can achieve the extraordinary, turning their collective efforts into the Midas touch that transforms the landscape of profitability.

Navigating Negotiations and Deal-Making

In the intricate dance of business, negotiations are the beating heart that fuels collaboration and growth. They are the conduits through which deals are forged, partnerships are solidified, and profits are maximized. Navigating negotiations and mastering the art of deal-making is an essential skill set that can elevate your business to unparalleled heights. In this sub-chapter, we will delve deep into the strategies that underpin successful negotiations, the principles of crafting win-win solutions, and the pivotal role of effective communication in sealing deals that generate lasting profitability.

Strategies for Successful Negotiations

Negotiation is both an art and a science, a delicate balance between asserting your interests while understanding the needs and aspirations of your counterpart. It requires meticulous preparation, clear objectives, and a strategic approach. Here are some key strategies to ensure your negotiations are on the path to success:

1. Preparation: The Keystone of Negotiation

Successful negotiations begin long before the meeting room. Research your counterpart's history, needs, and pain points. Understand your own bottom line and prioritize your goals. Anticipate potential objections and devise responses that highlight the value you bring.

2. Active Listening and Empathy

Effective negotiators are adept listeners. By truly understanding the concerns and aspirations of your counterpart, you can tailor your proposals to resonate with their needs. Empathy builds rapport, fostering an atmosphere of collaboration rather than confrontation.

3. Leveraging Alternatives and BATNA

Your Best Alternative to a Negotiated Agreement (BATNA) is your fallback position if the current negotiation fails. Knowing your BATNA gives you leverage and confidence, allowing you to walk away from deals that don't meet your criteria.

Win-Win Solutions and Value Maximization

In the realm of modern business, the concept of win-win has transcended buzzword status to become a guiding principle for sustainable success. A win-win solution transcends immediate financial gain and seeks to create value for all parties involved. This approach fosters trust and paves the way for enduring partnerships. Here's how to achieve a win-win outcome:

1. Focus on Interests, Not Positions

Look beyond the surface-level demands of both sides. Identify the underlying interests and motivations driving the negotiation. This opens doors to creative solutions that satisfy both parties' needs.

2. Value Creation through Collaboration

True value is often found in collaborative efforts. Seek opportunities to combine resources, knowledge, and expertise to create something greater than the sum of its parts. A collaborative mindset breeds goodwill and paves the way for future ventures.

Sealing Profitable Deals through Effective Communication

Communication is the glue that binds negotiations, turning concepts into tangible agreements. The ability to articulate your value proposition, understand your counterpart's perspective, and find common ground is paramount. Here's how effective communication seals profitable deals:

1. Clarity and Precision

Ambiguity breeds misunderstanding. Clearly articulate your terms, expectations, and benefits. Avoid jargon that may confuse or alienate your counterpart. Be concise, specific, and direct.

2. Building Rapport and Trust

Strong business relationships are built on trust. Share relevant information transparently and ethically. Highlight shared values and common objectives to foster rapport. A trustworthy image enhances your negotiation position.

3. Negotiation as a Dialog, Not a Monolog

A negotiation is a two-way street. Encourage open dialogue by asking open-ended questions. Listen actively and respond thoughtfully. Acknowledge your counterpart's input and incorporate it into your proposals.

In the intricate realm of deal-making, the dance of negotiation requires finesse, empathy, and strategic thinking. By honing your negotiation skills, creating value for all parties, and mastering the art of effective communication, you possess the Midas Touch to turn negotiations into transformative opportunities for profitable growth. Remember, negotiations are not battles to be won or lost; they are bridges to collaboration, innovation, and long-term prosperity. Through these principles, you can carve your path to unprecedented success, leaving behind a

trail of profitable deals and enduring partnerships that
define your business legacy.

Chapter 15: The Future of Profitable Business

Embracing Technological Advancements

In the ever-evolving landscape of modern business, the winds of change are often powered by technological advancements that reshape industries, disrupt traditional models, and offer unprecedented opportunities for profit. The advent of emerging technologies has given rise to a new era of innovation and transformation, where businesses have the chance to not only survive but thrive by harnessing the power of these tools. In this sub-chapter, we delve into the profound impact of emerging technologies on business, the strategic integration of AI, automation, and IoT for profit, and the art of staying ahead of the tech trends to maintain a competitive advantage.

Impact of Emerging Technologies on Business

The fabric of business is being rewoven by the threads of innovation. Emerging technologies, such as artificial intelligence (AI), blockchain, automation, and the Internet of Things (IoT), are revolutionizing how organizations operate, connect with customers, and make strategic decisions. The digitization of business processes is not merely a technological shift; it's a paradigm shift that requires a fundamental rethinking of business models, strategies, and mindsets.

Consider the role of AI, which empowers businesses to analyze massive datasets, predict customer behavior, automate routine tasks, and even enhance decision-making through advanced algorithms. The insights garnered from AI-driven analytics enable businesses to tailor products and services precisely to customer preferences, creating personalized experiences that lead to increased loyalty and profitability. Similarly, the integration of IoT devices allows businesses to collect real-time data from interconnected devices, optimizing supply chains, enhancing product development, and even enabling predictive maintenance in manufacturing processes.

Incorporating AI, Automation, and IoT for Profit
The true Midas Touch in today's business landscape is the ability to leverage AI, automation, and IoT to drive profits. The strategic implementation of these technologies can lead to operational efficiencies, cost savings, and enhanced customer experiences that directly impact the bottom line. Let's break down how each of these elements contributes to profit growth:

Artificial Intelligence (AI): AI has moved beyond sci-fi dreams to become a practical tool for businesses. By analyzing patterns and making data-driven predictions, AI can guide decision-makers toward optimal choices. Marketing efforts become laser-focused, inventory management becomes more precise, and customer interactions become increasingly personalized.

Automation: Automating repetitive tasks not only reduces human error but also frees up human resources for more strategic activities. From chatbots handling customer queries to robotic process automation streamlining administrative processes, automation is the silent profit enhancer that allows businesses to scale without a proportionate increase in costs.

Internet of Things (IoT): The interconnectedness of devices through IoT opens the door to real-time data collection and analysis. This enables businesses to optimize processes, improve product quality, and even create new revenue streams through data-based services. For instance, a manufacturing plant equipped with IoT sensors can monitor equipment health, allowing for predictive maintenance that minimizes downtime and maximizes productivity.

Staying Ahead of Tech Trends for Competitive Advantage
In the fast-paced world of business, standing still is akin to moving backward. To maintain a competitive edge, it's imperative to not only adopt existing technologies but also anticipate upcoming trends. The technology landscape is marked by constant evolution, and the ability to spot emerging trends and seize the first-mover advantage is a hallmark of successful businesses.

Continuous Learning and Adaptation: The embrace of technological advancements requires a culture of continuous learning and adaptation. Business leaders must invest in upskilling their teams to understand and leverage these technologies effectively. This involves a commitment to ongoing training, workshops, and a keen interest in the evolving tech landscape.

Exploration and Experimentation: Businesses that thrive in the future are those that embrace experimentation. It's important to allocate resources for exploring new technologies, testing their applicability to your business, and making calculated bets on their potential benefits.

Collaboration and Open Innovation: The pace of technology often outpaces individual business capacities. Collaborating with startups, tech firms, and research institutions can provide access to cutting-edge solutions and ideas. Embracing open innovation models allows businesses to harness external expertise and stay at the forefront of tech trends.

The future of profitable business is inextricably linked to the ability to embrace and harness technological advancements. The impact of emerging technologies is reshaping industries, and those who strategically integrate AI, automation, and IoT stand to reap substantial profits. Staying ahead of tech trends requires a commitment to continuous learning, exploration, and collaboration. By embracing the Midas Touch of technology, businesses can unlock new levels of profitability and position themselves as leaders in an increasingly digital world. As you embark on this technological journey, remember that the true value of these tools lies not in their complexity, but in their capacity to amplify your business's innate potential for success.

Entrepreneurial Mindset for Continuous Profit Growth

In the rapidly evolving landscape of business, the future belongs to those who embrace an entrepreneurial mindset—a mindset that transcends industry boundaries and propels individuals and organizations toward continuous profit growth. This sub-chapter delves into the core tenets of fostering adaptability, overcoming the paralyzing fear of failure, and cultivating an unwavering commitment to lifelong learning.

Fostering Adaptability and Innovation

In an era where change is the only constant, adaptability emerges as a cornerstone of sustainable profitability. The most successful entrepreneurs and business leaders are those who can swiftly pivot in response to market shifts and technological advancements. They anticipate disruption, rather than merely reacting to it.

Adaptability is rooted in an openness to new ideas and an eagerness to experiment. Embracing innovation not only invigorates business operations but also enhances value propositions for customers. Adaptable entrepreneurs actively seek feedback, iterate on their strategies, and drive the evolution of their products and services. By nurturing a culture of adaptability, businesses can ride the waves of change rather than be engulfed by them.

Overcoming Fear of Failure for Entrepreneurial Success
The fear of failure is a sentiment that looms large in the entrepreneurial journey. However, the most successful entrepreneurs have found a way to reframe failure as a stepping stone to success. They recognize that each setback carries valuable lessons and insights that propel them forward.

Overcoming the fear of failure requires a mindset shift. Instead of dwelling on the potential negatives, successful entrepreneurs focus on the positives—the knowledge gained, the resilience built, and the growth achieved. They understand that failure is not the end but a necessary part of the process. This perspective empowers them to take calculated risks, innovate boldly, and seize opportunities that others might shy away from.

Cultivating a Lifelong Learning Attitude
In the realm of business, stagnation is a harbinger of decline. Entrepreneurs who thrive in the future cultivate a lifelong learning attitude that keeps them perpetually curious and intellectually engaged. This attitude extends beyond formal education—it encompasses continuous self-improvement, seeking out mentors, attending workshops, and voraciously consuming information.

Lifelong learners recognize that the business landscape evolves rapidly, and success hinges on staying ahead of the curve. They eagerly explore emerging technologies, study industry trends, and identify novel ways to apply new knowledge. This commitment to learning fuels innovation, enables them to identify gaps in the market, and empowers them to pivot their strategies proactively.

The future of profitable business hinges on the foundation of an entrepreneurial mindset. Entrepreneurs who prioritize adaptability, overcome the fear of failure, and embrace lifelong learning are poised to navigate the ever-changing landscape with confidence and finesse. As an entrepreneur, embracing these principles positions you not merely as an observer of change, but as a proactive architect of the future.

Incorporating these principles into your business strategy positions you for resilience and prosperity, regardless of the challenges that may arise. The entrepreneurial journey is one of growth, evolution, and continuous refinement. By fostering adaptability, embracing failure as a springboard, and cultivating a passion for ongoing learning, you're not only shaping your business's destiny but also setting a transformative example for the broader entrepreneurial community.

Leaving a Legacy of Profitable Impact

In the journey of achieving and sustaining profitability in business, there comes a point when entrepreneurs and business leaders begin to consider their broader impact on society. Beyond the balance sheets and profit margins, the concept of leaving a lasting legacy of profitable impact gains prominence. This sub chapter delves into the importance of balancing financial success with giving back, the role of philanthropy and social contributions, and the strategies for sustaining a profitable impact for generations to come.

Balancing Financial Success with Giving Back
As businesses flourish and profits accumulate, the question of what to do with that success becomes increasingly significant. The idea of balancing financial success with giving back goes beyond the notion of corporate social responsibility. It reflects the realization that businesses have the power to be catalysts for positive change in their communities and the world at large. Balancing financial success with giving back is not about diminishing profits; rather, it's about recognizing that sustainable profitability can be intertwined with purpose-driven actions.

Business leaders often find that embracing a broader purpose beyond profit can actually enhance their reputation and attract customers who share their values. This alignment creates a positive feedback loop where doing good leads to increased profitability. Many successful entrepreneurs have witnessed that customers are more likely to support companies that demonstrate a commitment to making the world a better place.

Philanthropy and Social Contributions

One of the most direct ways for businesses to leave a legacy of profitable impact is through philanthropy and social contributions. These actions involve allocating a portion of profits, resources, or time towards initiatives that benefit society. Philanthropy is not just about writing a check; it's about strategically investing in projects and causes that align with the company's values and strengths.

Businesses can engage in various forms of philanthropy, such as supporting education, healthcare, environmental conservation, or community development. This involvement not only generates positive PR but also creates a sense of purpose and fulfillment among employees. When employees see that their work contributes to something greater than just profit, their commitment and satisfaction levels increase, further enhancing the company's overall performance.

Sustaining Profitable Impact for Generations

While philanthropy can create an immediate positive impact, sustaining profitable impact for generations requires a more comprehensive approach. This involves integrating social and environmental considerations into the core business strategy. Forward-thinking companies are recognizing that addressing societal challenges can actually lead to new business opportunities and revenue streams.

Sustainable business practices, such as adopting eco-friendly manufacturing processes, reducing waste, and supporting fair labor practices, not only benefit the environment and society but also enhance long-term profitability. Consumers are increasingly favoring companies that demonstrate social and environmental responsibility, and investors are valuing businesses with strong sustainability practices.

To sustain profitable impact for generations, companies must prioritize innovation that aligns with societal needs. By anticipating and adapting to changing trends, businesses can remain relevant and continue to provide value to their customers while positively impacting society.

 Leaving a legacy of profitable impact goes beyond financial success; it's about contributing to a better world through strategic actions that benefit both the business and society. Balancing financial success with giving back not only enhances reputation but also generates a sense of purpose and fulfillment. Philanthropy and social contributions allow businesses to make immediate positive changes, while sustainable practices and innovation ensure a long-lasting impact. By embracing this approach, entrepreneurs and business leaders can create a legacy that extends far beyond the boardroom, leaving a mark on society and the business landscape for generations to come.

Epilogue: The Unending Journey of Profitable Success

As we come to the closing chapter of "Midas Touch Secret: Strategy to Turn Any Business Profitable," it's essential to reflect on the remarkable journey we've undertaken together. We've explored the intricate landscape of business strategies, financial management, innovation, and sustainable practices, all aimed at unraveling the secrets behind turning any business into a profitable venture. Yet, our journey doesn't culminate here; instead, it serves as a stepping stone into the unending trajectory of profitable success.

The Evolution of Profitability: A Continual Unfolding
The world of business is in constant flux, marked by shifting market dynamics, technological breakthroughs, and evolving customer preferences. Profitability, too, is not a fixed destination but rather an ongoing pursuit that demands adaptability, innovation, and a willingness to embrace change. As entrepreneurs and business leaders, our journey to profitability is a continual unfolding—one that requires us to stay attuned to the pulse of our industry, anticipate trends, and foster a culture of curiosity and learning.

The Power of Iteration and Resilience
In the pursuit of profitability, setbacks and challenges are inevitable. However, what sets successful businesses apart is their capacity to iterate, adapt, and rebound stronger than before. The ability to transform failures into stepping stones toward success is a hallmark of resilient entrepreneurs. Remember, the path to profitability is not always linear, but each challenge you overcome contributes to your growth and the fortification of your business.

Sustaining the Flame of Purpose
While profitability is undeniably crucial for business sustainability, it is equally important to maintain a burning flame of purpose that guides your journey. Beyond the pursuit of profits, ask yourself: What legacy do you want to leave? How can your business contribute positively to society and the lives it touches? Aligning your purpose with your profitability efforts can infuse your work with deeper meaning, fostering an environment where profits and purpose are intertwined.

Embracing the Adventure of Innovation
Innovation is the lifeblood of profitable businesses. It's about challenging norms, exploring uncharted territories, and envisioning new ways to meet customer needs. As we move forward, remember that innovation isn't confined to product development; it extends to every facet of your business, from processes and marketing to customer experiences. The ability to innovate and adapt ensures that

your business remains relevant and resilient in a rapidly changing world.

Cultivating a Learning Mindset

The business landscape is an ever-evolving ecosystem, and to thrive, we must embrace a continuous learning mindset. Stay curious, seek out new knowledge, and remain open to perspectives beyond your own. Surround yourself with mentors, peers, and resources that inspire growth. A learning mindset fuels your ability to anticipate trends, understand emerging technologies, and make informed decisions that drive profitability.

The Unending Quest for Balance

As you tread the path of profitability, remember that success extends beyond the balance sheet. Strive to find balance in your life, ensuring that your pursuit of profitability doesn't come at the cost of your well-being, relationships, or values. A harmonious life provides you with the clarity and energy needed to steer your business toward sustainable profitability.

A New Beginning, Every Day

In closing, dear reader, remember that the journey to profitable success is not confined to the pages of this book. It is a narrative that you continue to write each day, with every decision and action. The principles, strategies, and insights shared within these chapters are the foundations upon which you can build a thriving business. But it's you—the visionary, the dreamer, the doer—who breathes life into these principles.

As you embark on your unending journey of profitable success, may your ventures be marked by purpose, resilience, innovation, and an unwavering commitment to continuous learning. The world of business eagerly awaits your contributions, your impact, and your legacy. May your pursuit of profitability be a beacon of inspiration to those who follow in your footsteps.